Valerie Crespí-Green

APR 1 9 2016 walk & eat
MALLORCA

CONTENTS

This pocket guide is designed for walking holidays on Mallorca with a gastronomical touch, using public transport. Mallorca, largest of the Balearic Isles, is one Europe's most popular holiday destinations and easily reached by air. Out of season, many airlines offer inexpensive daily flights to the island — just when walking is at its best. Whether you plan just a short break or a longer holiday, you'll find plenty to do in this book. Mix together the following ingredients to make this a great little holiday:

- 10 varied full or half-day walks, each with topographical map
- 2 excursions — 1 long trip by train, tram and boat, the other a train ride to the centre of the island
- recommended restaurants and hotels
- recipes to try out at your self-catering base or back home
- special section with hints on wheat-, gluten- and dairy-free eating and cooking on the island

INTRO

THE WALKS

The walks in this book range from gentle low-level walking to more strenuous mountain hikes; all can be done by anyone who is reasonably fit. They are all accessible by public transport, with good eating either at the beginning, en route or at the finish. For a wider range of walking possibilities I recommend *Landscapes of Mallorca*, also published by Sunflower Books.

Landscapes of Mallorca was first published in 1984, the second book to be published in the *Landscapes* series. It opened up the island to many surprised visitors who considered Mallorca to be just another 'sun and beach' destination, re-discovering the island for thousands of tourists and winning an 'Oscar' from the *Sunday Times*. Now in its eighth edition, *Landscapes of Mallorca* is widely used by visitors (and residents!), and has proved to be a valuable reference for the travel press. The 'Landscapes' series now covers 50 destinations. For more information see www.sunflowerbooks.co.uk.

THE EXCURSIONS

One trip is a good full day's outing using the quaint little 'wild west' train to Sóller, then tram to the port, and finally boat to one of the most stunning and grandiose enclaves on Mallorca's north coast, the Sa Calobra gorge.

The second excursion is by train to Inca, at the centre of the island, where a huge outdoor market selling anything you can imagine fills the streets every Thursday morning. End the trip with a meal at one of Inca's typical *celler* restaurants.

THE RESTAURANTS

Mallorca has so many restaurants that you'd be hard put to go far without seeing one! You will find good restaurants at the start or finish of all the walks. Some walks include a mid-way meal — whether at a mountain refuge, monastery or restaurant. All restaurants have been chosen for their walker-friendliness (don't mind dirty boots!), beautiful surroundings or, naturally, for the good food they serve. In each case I show a 'mini-menu', listing some of their specialities. Also, a price guide is given (€ to €€€) to indicate 'very reasonable' to 'fairly pricey'. At most of the restaurants mentioned you can get a fairly economical meal, where the choice of a local wine will not push the price up too much.

Mallorca does, by the way, produce some excellent wines; one of my favourites is an ecological red called 'Carmesí', from the Jaume de Puntiró wine *celler* in Santa Maria. For example: two people can enjoy *sopas Mallorquinas* and a *pa amb oli* with a half-litre jug of red wine sitting on the leafy terrace of Es Turó in Fornalutx for under 20 € — and that includes the view!

THE RECIPES

Nearly everyone was willing to share recipes with me, in fact the eagerness of some to share personal little tips or secrets surprised me to say the least!

None of the recipes in this book are difficult. Most of them use easily obtainable local produce found in market places or supermarkets. So you can try some of them while at your self-catering base, or even back home, bearing in mind that they will obviously taste better when prepared on the spot with local ingredients. It is difficult to transfer some recipes to another country with complete success, since so many factors determine the outcome — the water, the soil, the freshness of the produce, etc.

While Mallorcans eat a good deal of pork, lamb and fish, they also have some good vegetarian dishes, for example *tumbet* (similar to ratatouille), or *trempó*, a fresh summer salad of peppers, onions and tomatoes.

Pa amb oli is *the* traditional Mallorcan dish. Here's how they serve it at Es Turó in Fornalutx. For the ingredients, see page 37!

Also, good news for people with food intolerances: all these recipes can be **gluten or dairy-free** (see page 138).

MALLORCAN FOOD

Mallorcan food is all about the Mediterranean diet: fresh vegetables and fruit, virgin olive oil, locally-caught fresh fish, mountain-reared lambs and goats, game, fresh herbs — you cannot eat more healthily!

Fresh **fish** is always available — a visit to the fresh fish market at the Mercat de l'Olivar in Palma is an experience in itself. **Lamb** and **pork** are the meat favourites; *lechona* (roast suckling pig) is a festive dish served at Christmas or weddings,

Suckling pig at Es Turó (Walk 1)

but also served in many restaurants. The roast lamb at Es Vergé (Walk 4) is especially good, like you've never tasted — slow-baked in an ancient stone oven until it falls of the bone. **Chicken** and **game** dishes such as partridge and rabbit also figure on most menus.

The Mallorcans are fond of rice dishes too, 'paella-style' or a particularly scrumptious soup version called *arròs brut* (dirty rice) — a rice broth full of chunks of pork, chicken, rabbit and vegetables; some recipes even add snails or locally picked *setas* (wild mushrooms). Another version would be *arròs de peix* – fish and rice soup, usually with fresh prawns and mussels.

And the Mallorcans don't get left behind when it comes to desserts — there's *coca d'ametla* (a home-made almond sponge cake), usually served with almond ice-cream, or *brossat*, a local type of cheesecake — not forgetting locally grown fresh seasonal fruits like apricots, loquats, oranges, grapes, or cherries.

You can't leave a Mallorcan restaurant without rounding off your meal with a tot of *herbes* (*hierbas* in Spanish — usually 'on the house') — otherwise you might offend the waiter! *Herbes* is a Mallorcan liqueur produced by steeping many different types of fresh wild herbs in an alcohol base, usually anise. It is a *digestif,* and the Mallorcans swear by it for warding off colds, 'flu and other ills. There are dry *(seques)* and sweet *(dolces)* versions.

MALLORCAN WINES

All the supermarkets stock a good selection of Spanish and international wines, including an ample variety of Mallorcan wines. In 1991, some Mallorcan wines — namely those produced from vines in and around the Binissalem area — were awarded the 'Denominació d'Origen' (D.O.), meaning that they are sampled and approved by a testing panel; this guarantees that the wine really does come from a specific area and has had to undergo strict controls. There are now two D.O. areas, Binissalem and Pla i Llevant. The Binissalem vineyards cover an extensive area on the central plain around the villages of Santa Maria, Consell, Santa Eugènia, Sencelles and Binissalem, whereas the Pla i Llevant D.O.s come from the eastern coast. You can find these D.O.s in shops and supermarkets.

However, not all locally produced wine is sold commercially; it's exciting to visit local wine cellars *(bodegas)* — nearly every village has one or more — and sample straight from the barrel before buying; obviously it's cheaper too. Wherever you see a sprig of greenery or a branch over an entrance, be assured that there are some huge wine vats lurking behind those doors!

You can also buy local wines in open-air markets. One of my favourites is an ecologically grown, sophisticated red called 'Carmesí', produced by Jaume de Puntiró. You can find it in some shops; if not, it is always on sale at the bodega at 23 Plaça

Nova (in the market square) at Santa Maria (℃ 971 620023, open from 9.00-13.00 on Saturdays and Sundays *only*).

Just at the entrance to Santa Eugènia, there is another bodega, Vinya Taujana (℃ 971 144494), owned by the Crespí family. They have been winemakers for over a hundred years and sell good local wines, including their own D.O.s, reds, whites and muscatels.

I also recommend the 'Santa Catarina' wines, based in Andratx (℃ 971 235413), but sold in most supermarkets. Macià Batle (℃ 971 140014) have taken over the marketing of Santa Catarina wines, and you can visit their bodega on the Ma13A in Santa Maria (near the railway station; see the map on page 73).

The grapes used to produce D.O.s come from the Manto Negro, Cabernet-Sauvignon, Fogoneu, Merlot, Calet, Tempranillo, Shiraz or Prensal Blanc varieties. Other varieties cultivated on the island are Monastrell, Giro Blanc, Gargollosa, Chardonnay, Muscat, Macabeo — and more.

PLANNING YOUR VISIT
When to go

It's best to avoid the hot summer months of July and August, when temperatures soar into the high 30°s (or even 40°s), and the humidity is high. Walk anytime during the rest of the year. Spring, when all the wild flowers are in bloom, is lovely, and the cool crisp days of winter are ideal. A popular time for walking in Mallorca is January to February, when the whole island is draped in a 'snowy' covering of almond blossom — their delicate pink and white flowers contrasted against an intense blue sky — and as these months are 'out of season', travelling is usually much cheaper and hotel rates more attractive.

Where to stay

There is a wide choice of hotels, villas and self-catering accommodation. Rural hotels and *agroturismos* — where you can come closer to the 'real' Mallorca — are plentiful,

On a winter walk near Tossals Verds (Walk 6)

but can be more expensive, and you usually need a hired car.

If you want to get about by public transport, Palma city is the best option, with many hotels. These range from luxurious 5-star establishments (often in historic buildings, such as the Palacio Galesa, a restored bishops' palace just behind the cathedral) to more modest seafront 3-star hotels, with accommodation from as little as 35 € per night. You can find a good selection at www.visit-palma.com. Some walks offer the opportunity for an overnight stay — at a monastery, mountain refuge or nearby hotel.

What to take

Unless you are staying at a 5-star hotel or one of the more elegant *agroturismos,* there is no need to pack elegant clothing.

All the restaurants I've mentioned won't mind you dining in your walking gear, so pack for comfort.

While no special equipment is needed for any of the walks, proper **walking boots** are preferable to any other footwear. Many walks can be wet or slippery at some stage; good ankle support is essential, and you will also be glad of the water-proofing. Each person should carry a **small rucksack**, and *all year round* it is advisable to pack it with a **sunhat, first-aid kit, spare socks** and some **warm clothing**. A **long-sleeved shirt** and **long trousers** should be worn or carried, for sun protection and for making your way through encroaching vegetation (which may be wet and prickly). You should always carry a **mobile phone**; the **emergency** number on Mallorca (as throughout the EU) is 112. *Note: some walks require a torch.*

Depending on the season, you may also need a **windproof, lightweight rainwear, fleece** and **gloves**. Optional items include **swimwear** and a Swiss Army knife (packed in your hold luggage, *not* hand-luggage, or it will be confiscated!). Mineral water is sold almost everywhere in plastic half-litre bottles; *it is imperative that each walker carries at least one litre of water — two litres in hot weather.*

Planning your walks

In this book you will find short walks, ideal for half-days out, as well as full-day hikes. Remember to allow time for your wining and dining adventures when arranging your transport times. All the walks are accessible by **public transport**, so that you can enjoy the wines! If you hire a car, remember that Spanish law is very strict on drinking and driving: the limit is 0.5mg/l — equivalent to two glasses of wine. At least four of the walks include a mid-walk meal, while the rest recommend restaurants at the start or finish, some at hotels where you might like to spend the night.

All the walks in this book can be done by anyone who is **reasonably fit**, as none is technically difficult, and none requires any specific equipment other than good walking shoes, preferably boots, and sensible clothing — basically a thermal/synthetic inner layer, shirt or fleece, and water/windproof top layer. My **walking times** are just that — purely *walking* times, so you should allow for photography stops, snacks, meals, etc when planning your day.

The **maps** in this book have been adapted from the latest 1:25,000 IGN and 1:50,000 military maps of the Balearics. These, and some good new maps from Editorial Alpina (1:25,000), are available locally at the Casa del Mapa, Carrer Santo Domingo Nº 11 in Palma (Mon-Fri 09.30-14.00; (971 225945).

All of these routes are well **waymarked**, some with GR *(grande route)* wooden signposts, others are indicated by cairns. **Walking safely** depends in great part on *knowing what to expect and being properly equipped*. So please read the whole walk description at your leisure *before* setting out, so that you have each stage of the route and landmarks in mind. You will usually meet other walkers on all these routes; however, I strongly advise you *never to walk alone.*

ON ARRIVAL
Tourist information

There is a tourist information office inside Palma airport (℆ 971 789556), also three in Palma itself, each highlighted with the number [1] on the plan inside the front cover: at the railway station park (℆ 971 754329), on the Passeig d'es Born north of Plaça de la Reina (℆ 971 724090), and the Tourist Board headquarters, the *Foment de Turisme*, on the first floor at Constitució Nº 1 (℆ 971 725396). There are also offices in Valldemossa, Sóller and Port Sóller.

Palma bus and railway station

The main bus and railway station (℆ 971 177777) is at Plaça d'Espanya just northeast of the 'Avingudas'. Opposite, across

Carrer Eusebi Estada, is the Sóller railway station (℆ 971 752051, 971 752028, 902 364711).

Timetables are available free at all tourist offices. For further information log on to www.mallorcaweb site.com, www. visitbalears.com, or the websites shown on page 137.

Relax with a morning coffee at Palma's railway station before boarding your train.

There is a city bus (Bus Ciudad) to and from Palma airport, going through Palma city centre every 15 minutes; this costs just 1,80 €. For other Palma city buses contact ℂ 971 177777 or pick up the latest timetable from one of the tourist offices.

Shopping for self-catering

Obviously your first port of call will be one of the big **hyper-markets** in Palma to stock up on all essentials. There are two Carrefour supermarkets in Palma, one at the Porto Pí Centre, at Avinguda Gabriel Roca 54 (at the western end of the Passeig Marítim; open 10.00-22.00 Mon-Sat and some holidays), and the other just off the Via Cintura (Valldemossa exit) at Avinguda General Riera 152 (open 09.30-21.30 Mon-Sat and some holi-days). Both are just outside the area covered by our plan.

If you have hired a car, there's a Carrefour hypermarket just by Palma airport: take the motorway exit for 'Coll d'en Rabassa'; it is well signposted (open 10.00-22.00 daily including holidays). Just inside this hypermarket, to the right, is a separate **health food store, Winoky's** (ℂ 971 745733), selling a wide range of gluten- and dairy-free products. There is also an Alcampo hypermarket on the Palma/Inca motorway: the exit is at km 3.9. Most of the bigger villages have a supermarket; 'Hipercentro', 'Mercadona', 'Caprabo' or 'Eroski SYP' are the most common. The Hipercentro in Inca is huge, and sells everything.

Regional produce

There is plenty of fresh fruit and vegetables on sale at open-air markets, local shops and supermarkets all year round. One of the best things about Mallorca is that there is always something fresh available! Oranges and clementines, almonds, cherries, apricots, market-garden produce such as peppers, all kinds of

Tempting display at Especias Crespí ...

greens, onions, garlic and root vegetables. Mallorca even grows its own rice!

Butchers sell local farm-reared lamb, pork, chicken and beef, as well as EU produce. You can distinguish local, ecologically grown products by the ticket with a logo reading 'Consell Balear de la Producció Agrària Ecològica' printed around a blue sky with a bright yellow sun, brown earth and green splashes.

Freshly-caught fish is always available, and a visit to the fresh fish market inside the Mercat de l'Olivar (13 on the plan) is a must!

For aromatic herbs, freshly ground *pimentón*, nuts and spices, visit **Especias Crespí**, just around the corner from the Mercat de L'Olivar: walk down Carrer Velazquez to the beginning of Via Sindicat, where they are at N° 64 ((971 715640; 27 on the plan).

Most villages hold an open-air agricultural market with locally grown fruit and vegetables. The most important are in

Santa Maria (Sunday mornings), Inca (Thursday mornings; see Excursion 2) and Sineu (Wednesday mornings; one of the oldest on the island, held every week since the Middle Ages).

If you have a hired car, you can buy fresh organic farm produce at the Finca Son Barrina (℃ 971 504540) on the Inca/Llubí road: coming from Inca, turn left just before the km 6 marker. Run by an English-speaking Canadian lady called Connie, who offers a wide range of grains, pastas and pulses, as well as fresh fruit and veg. Or visit Bio Mallorca in Llucmajor (Ronda de Ponent N° 66; telephone before visiting ℃ 971 660082), a great place for organic vegetarian food — especially their home-made olive paté.

... and at the Mercat d'Olivar

Virtually all supermarkets have a **health-food** section, where you can buy soya or rice milk, tofus, grains etc — usually the Gerblé, Provamel or Santiveri brands. There are also plenty of 'natural foods' shops in Palma, some of which sell gluten-free products (see overleaf for a selection of handy, well-stocked shops).

Health food shops in Palma

The handiest is **Murta** — just across from the Mercat de L'Olivar: leave by the fish market exit, cross over to the Geranis Centre, then veer slightly right along the passageway called Santa Catalina de Siena.

Straight ahead you'll see Murta (Comercial Los Geranios, 22 on the plan; (971 710 202). Here you will find all the GF and DF ingredients you need. They stock the wide range of Glutano and Proceli products, as well as two other brands, Campesina and Sorribas.

Both branches of **El Corte Inglés**, Mallorca's large department stores (26 on the plan), have health food sections stocking the usual dairy-free products and Schär gluten-free breads, cakes, biscuits, pastas, etc. These are at Avinguda Alexandre Rosselló, 12-16 and Avinguda Jaime III, 15 ((971 770177 for both stores). Open 09.30-21.30 daily including holidays.

The Schär website claims that their products are also sold at the shops listed below. I have not personally checked these, so it would be wise to *phone ahead*. If they *do* sell Schär, it's certain that they will have other suppliers and sell most of the gf, df products you may be looking for.

Farmacia Clar, Plaça Orson Welles, 4 ((971 272212)

Mallorca Natural, Avinguda Argentina, 10 ((971 451034)

Rincón de las Hierbas, Avinguda Joan Miró, 155 (Sant Augustí) ((971 405216)

Farmacia Maria del Carmen Aguiló, Metge Josep Darder, 24 ((971 276453)

Finally, if you have a car, don't forget **Winoky's** at the Carrefour near the airport (see page 15).

Mercat de L'Olivar

This huge, recently restored indoor market (13 on the plan; (971 720314) is located in Plaça de l'Olivar just south-west of Plaça d'Espanya. It's open from 07.00-14.30 Monday to Saturday, and on Fridays it stays open until 20.00; closed Sundays. Coffee bars will take the weight off your feet and provide respite from the colourful thronging multitudes.

There is fresh produce every day — fruit, vegetables, meat and fish, plus healthfood shops — in short, almost everything you could ever need.

You *must* visit the adjacent fresh fish market, if only for the experience of seeing staggering quantities of all types of seafood and freshly-caught fish — and, if you're good at bargaining, at an equally staggering price!

A fabulous all-day trip! The train from Palma carries you across the plain towards the Tramuntana mountain range, down into the pretty valley of Sóller, from where you travel by tram to the port. From here, a boat ride past Mallorca's rugged northern coastline brings you to the stunning scenery of the Sa Calobra gorge.

sa calobra

EXCURSION

To take advantage of all that this excursion has to offer, you need to take the early train to Sóller; this allows you time to visit Sant Bartomeu Church or the botanical gardens in Sóller before continuing to the Port. If weather is not permitting boats out to Sa Calobra, then the maritime museum is the next best thing!

The excursion begins in Palma's **Plaça d'Espanya** at the **Sóller railway station**. The wooden carriages, 'wild-west' style, rattle out of Palma straight down the centre of the main road and out of the city, heading between almond and olive orchards towards the Tramuntana mountain range. After **Bunyola** (Walk 3), a mountain village full of steps, the train delves deep into a 3km-long tunnel, emerging

Transport: ⚞ from Palma to Sóller (daily 08.00, 10.45); journey time 1h; connects with the 🚋 to Port Sóller (every 30min/hourly in winter). ⚓ leaves the jetty (from the last tram stop, by the Marisol Restaurant) at 10.00, 11.00, 13.00; sailing time 45min. ⚓ returns from Sa Calobra *only* at 14.00, 16.30; last train departs Sóller at 18.00 (summer also 19.00)

Refreshments en route:
Palma station café (see page 14)
El Guía hotel and restaurant (Sóller)
Lua restaurant (Port Sóller)

Points of Interest:
Sóller railway station (built 1606)
Sant Bartomeu church in Sóller
Sóller Botanical Gardens and Natural Science Museum, open 10:00-18:00 Mon-Sat (Mar-Oct), 10:00-14:00 (Nov-Feb); cl Sun/holidays, also Mon from Nov-Feb. ℂ 971 634064; e-mail: musbcn@teleline.es; www. jardibotanicdesoller.org
Museu de la Mar, Port Sóller, open daily except Mon from 10:00-14:00 and 17:00-20:00 (Sun 10.00-14.00 only). ℂ 971 630200
See map on pages 134-135.

later on the northern side high above the beautiful sheltered Sóller Valley. This amazingly engineered railway carries the train down from the heights through a series of shorter tunnels

The Sóller Railway
The Sóller railway was officially inaugurated on 16th April 1912 (the day after the Titanic sank). Work began on the line in 1905, beginning simultaneously at both ends, until they met up in 1911. It was electrified on 14th July 1929.
The railway station in Sóller is without doubt one of the oldest in Europe. The building, known as Ca'n Mayol, dates from 1606; the columns below the station, shown above, still survive from that time. It was transformed into a railway station in 1911 — the year the railway excavations met up inside the tunnel.

and down into **Sóller** itself. The parked wagon beside the tramlines is Sóller's original tourist office, should you need to pick up any of the latest timetables. Just below the station steps, a clanging bell announces the arrival of the little orange tram, connecting to the port some three kilometres away.

However, why not explore Sóller first? Just a hundred metres down from the station (see plan on page 31) you come to the colourful **Plaça de Sa Constitució**, dominated by the enormous parish church of **Sant Bartomeu**, built around 1230. After several modifications, the baroque structure (with neo-Gothic tower) now dates from 1688. Some 16th-century walls still stand, as well as the Romanic porches. The immense façade was designed by Joan Rubí in 1904. The square itself, filled with colourful cafés, bustles with mingling tourists, walkers and residents alike.

Heading back towards the station, go right on Carrer

Isabel II and continue up to a bend to the left, then go right, past the 18th-century baroque church and convent and up the lane. You emerge on the main road to the port, just above the **Jardí Botanic de Sóller**. Even if you are not interested in botany, you'll be amazed at what this place has to offer; a walk round the beautifully set out gardens and lily ponds lets you discover a multitude of endemic and other Mediterranean plants in an intensely peaceful atmosphere.

The Sóller Tram
The tramline was inaugurated on the 11th October 1913 and was the first tram in Mallorca to run on electricity. Three wagons were built, and at a later date five more were bought from Lisbon. The Posada de l'Artesà, an old building still standing at the end of the tramline, was the station from where horse-drawn coaches used to leave for Palma city in bygone days.

From here walk back to the Plaça de Sa Constitució and take the tram through the back-street gardens of Sóller, past oranges and lemons hanging at arm's reach, down to Sóller's perfectly round, picturesque port. The tram goes all the way round beside the water before stopping at the Marisol Restaurant — just by the jetty where the boats leave for Sa Calobra (tickets can be bought on the jetty).

The big boat rides over the calm, protected waters of the bay and out onto open sea, veering north. The scenery is absolutely spectacular. After passing the lighthouse and a 16th-century

Museu de la Mar
This sea museum has been built inside the **Oratory of Santa Catalina**. The oratory was originally built in 1280, but destroyed by pirates in 1542 and rebuilt in 1550. From up here you have a wonderful view over the port. The large red boat is the one that goes to Sa Calobra.

watchtower, the vertical rugged limestone cliffs rise ever higher out of the sea forming chasms, torrent outlets and hidden coves. Even more imposing is the entry to **Sa Calobra**, near the **Torrent de Pareis gorge**. After heavy rains, a double torrent (*pareis* = a pair) cascades down from the mountains between the vertical cliffs of this gorge, before emptying out into the sea by a small shingle beach. To reach this exciting spot, go left from the jetty where you docked and through two rock tunnels — even explore up the gorge if you have time. But remember to be back well in time for your boat departure!

On rough or stormy winter days the Sa Calobra boats will not be running. A good alternative is to continue 200-300m round the port on foot and then have an excellent lunch at **Lua**, that lovely lemon-coloured building on the corner with splendid views across the bay. But first climb the flight of steps up to the **Museu de la Mar** inside the Oratory of Santa Catarina d'Alexandría. The sea and sailing has played a very important part in Port Sóller's history, and you will find this visit surprisingly interesting.

Jardi Botanic de Sóller

Return to Sóller by tram and choose between a return train ride or bus ride back to the city. Or have a delicious dinner of Mallorcan cuisine at **El Guía** — a little hotel and restaurant known locally as 'Ca's Pentinadó', and enjoy a peaceful overnight stay in Sóller — ideal if you want to try Walk 1 tomorrow!

Lua

You'll be glad you chose Lua for lunch! On the slopes of Santa Catalina, just below the steps to the oratory and museum, this restaurant has excellent views over the port from the upstairs dining room or the rooftop terrace. There are starter courses, soups, fish, meat and vegetable dishes. These, and some of their wonderful desserts, are shown on their mouth-watering website.

LUA
C/ Santa Catalina Nº 1
07108 Port Sóller (971 634745
www.restaurantelua.es
daily ex Mon, lunch and dinner
€-€€

specialities include **house salad** (see recipe on page 29), **fresh fish** (delivered daily at noon and always served with oven-roast potatoes), **biscuit glacé** (a Christmas recipe; see page 29) or **crêpes** sauced with Sóller oranges and Gran Marnier and filled with fruit and nuts

restaurants

eat

El Guía

Next to Sóller railway station (with your back to the station, go left at bottom of the station steps) you'll find El Guía, locally called 'Ca's Pentinadó'. It was founded in 1880 as a 'classic restaurant and petit hotel' and is still run by the same family. You may want to stay overnight — but there are only 18 rooms, so it's a good idea to book ahead.

This 'olde worlde'-style building is worth visiting even if you don't stop to eat; you'll love the pretty little outdoor patio with its stone well in the centre. And the entrance has not changed — antique furniture and well-worn leather chairs are reminiscent of the atmosphere of a small 19th-century hotel.

Bernardino has been a waiter here for over 42 years, and the present owner is over 90 years old! If fresh produce cannot be obtained daily from the local market, they will not prepare certain dishes.

Courtyard and dining room at El Guía, a lovely place to spend the night

EL GUIA
C/ Castanyer N° 2, 07100 Sóller
(971 630227/fax 971 632634
daily lunch and dinner (closed Mon in winter) €€-€€€

specialities include home-made vegetable **soup**, **squids** in garlic, stuffed **artichokes** and fresh **mandarin sorbet**

Jaime, the chef at El Guía, has managed to keep his recipes secret for over 30 years! However, I tried inventing my own recipe for the stuffed artichokes, as they seemed an uncomplicated dish, and they turned out beautifully! Here's how I prepare them.

Stuffed artichokes (carxofes farcides)

Cut off the stems and tops of the artichokes, and steam them, but do not let them get too soft. Remove the fibrous 'choke' and discard.

Cook and drain the spinach, and mash it up finely with the pine nuts and a little cream to make a paste. Fill the artichokes with this paste and set aside, keeping warm.

To make the sauce, peel the tomatoes and chop finely; stir-fry them in a little olive oil and add the garlic. Finally add the chopped parsley, and simmer gently until it becomes a sauce.

Pour sauce over each artichoke, sprinkle some grated cheese on top, and place under the grill until browned.

Ingredients (for 4 people)
8 artichokes
bunch of fresh spinach
small amount fresh cream
pine nuts to taste
six large ripe tomatoes
1-2 garlic cloves, crushed
fresh parsley (my own touch)
grated cheese
olive oil
salt and pepper

recipes

eat

Lua's house salad

Arrange the lettuce and endive on a plate; decorate with the orange slices and cheese, then sprinkle several whole walnuts over the top. Shake up all the vinaigrette ingredients vigorously, and pour over the salad before serving.

Lua's biscuit glacé (only served in the Christmas season)

Beat together the egg yolks and sugar in a 'bain marie' (double boiler) for about 10min, until the sugar melts. Then add the dried figs and the orange liqueur. Stir for another 10min, then add the honey.

Let the mixture cool, whip up the cream and mix in; pour into a mould and freeze for 12 hours. Serve in slices, with hot chocolate sauce dribbled on top.

Ingredients (for 4 people)
4 Sóller oranges, peeled and
  sliced
50 g whole walnuts
200 g Menorcan or Mallorcan
  cheese, diced
lettuce & endive leaves
for the vinaigrette:
2/3 Sóller olive oil
1/3 balsamic vinegar
1 tbsp Sóller honey
1 tsp mustard (with seeds)

Ingredients (for 4 people)
6 egg yolks, lightly beaten
1 teaspoons sugar
200 ml fresh cream
200 g dried figs, diced
1 shot glass of orange liqueur
4-5 tsp Sóller honey
dark chocolate, melted

This is a stunningly beautiful circular walk, deep in the Sóller valley, among heavily laden orange and lemon trees and a myriad of olive groves, surrounded by the island's highest peaks. Have lunch on the terrace at Es Turó, overlooking the picturesque village of Fornalutx, then return to Sóller via the opposite side of the valley.

biniaraix and fornalutx

WALK

1

The walk starts from the **Plaça de Sa Constitució** in **Sóller**, just below the railway station. With your back to the church, follow narrow **Carrer de Sa Lluna** to the right. At the crossroads by a bridge (**10min**) keep straight ahead for 'Biniaraix'. Just a few metres along you come to the big old Mallorcan house of **Ca'n Det**, where olive oil has been cold-pressed for over 300 years.

Distance/time: 7km/4.3mi; 3h

Grade: easy-moderate, with an ascent of 250m/820ft; gentle gradients

Equipment: walking boots or shoes, sunhat, suncream, camera, water

Transport: 🚂 or 🚌 L211 to/from Sóller (see pages 21 and 137)

Refreshments en route:
Bar Bodega in Biniaraix for freshly-squeezed orange juice or coffee
Restaurant Es Turó in Fornalutx

Points of interest:
Sóller (see page 21)
Ca'n Det, olive oil press and bodega

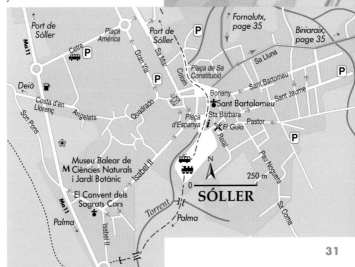

31

Ca'n Det
Carrer d'Ozones 8, Sóller
℡ 971 630303; e: candet@eresmas.net

This beautiful old Mallorcan town house hides an enormous olive press, where olives picked from the nearby mountain slopes have been cold-pressed for hundreds of years. The family has been pressing oil for over 300 years, still using the old traditional methods, although recently introduced EU laws obliged them to change the donkey for more modern, electrically driven machinery. They have their own olive groves, but also press oil for smaller farms.

They will be more than willing to show you round — through the big old house, out into the back patio, and through a narrow door into the huge oil-pressing warehouse, where you can watch the oil being pressed — if you are lucky enough to be passing through from December to February. Otherwise, you can see a video about olive oil production, and also sample some on a *pa amb oli*, the traditional bread and oil with tomato served in all Mallorcan homes.

You can also buy elegant bottles of cold-pressed oil from their 'shop' down the steps in a cool underground cellar, the ideal place for preserving all the qualities of this excellent local product.

Keeping ahead, the lane soon crosses a **bridge** (**25min**) and winds up to **Biniaraix**, where you take the stone steps up left on the S-bend. Then follow cobbled steps, turning right past quaint little stone houses up to the tiny village square, dominated by a large plane tree. You might see other walkers here, enjoying some refreshment at **Bar Bodega** — the freshly squeezed juice from oranges straight off the tree is ideal on a hot day!

Continue past Bar Bodega and straight ahead along **Carrer de Sant Josep**; at the end, go right, past the old stone **wash-house**. Just behind the washhouse, take the narrow tarmac

Biniaraix, and Bar Bodega

lane off left (**Camí del Marroig**). This quiet country lane winds uphill, fairly steeply at times, between beautiful olive tree terraces, affording splendid panoramic views back down over the Sóller valley. Higher up, Fornalutx comes into view from time to time over to the left, nestling at the head of a valley. As the lane winds up and up, you will marvel at the precision of these beautiful drystone terrace walls.

Just after a sharp but long S-bend, a wooden signpost at the left of the lane indicates 'Fornalutx a peu' (Fornalutx on foot; **1h20min**). Go down the rough stone steps, past another rudimentary signpost, after which you zigzag down the slopes, to descend

The 'ancient stone steps' from the Camí del Marroig — I'm almost at the bottom

more ancient stone steps. You come onto a tarmac lane, the **Camí d'es Creue**. Turn left for the final decent into **Fornalutx (1h50min)**. Once at the bottom, go left again along **Carrer de Sa Font** — almost to the end — and then go up the narrow steps onto the main village road. Turn right uphill and in a few minutes you'll come to the beautiful terraced restaurant of **Es Turó** (see page 37).

From the restaurant, walk downhill towards the village, to the small **square** (where there is usually a fruit display on the corner by the supermarket). Fornalutx is so picturesque that you might want to explore up the wide stone steps off to the right before continuing: they climb way up the hillside, with breathtaking views over Fornalutx and its backcloth of high mountains.

From the square continue along the narrow paved alley (**Carrer de Sa Plaça**), veering left downhill at the end and then right, along the railed **Carrer Joan Albertí Arbona**. Pass some **tennis courts** on the right and keep ahead; soon you will see some **GR** (Grande Route) signposts to 'Sóller' and 'Binibassi'. The lane continues out of the village and passes the small

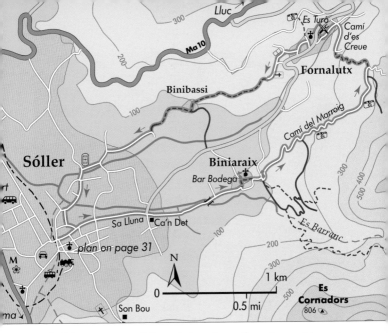

walled-in **cemetery** of Fornalutx, where there is a wide rest area. A few minutes later the lane ends, but the (signposted) route continues up to the right — a narrow rocky path between holm oaks and carob trees. You are now on the original, centuries-old wayfarers' route between Sóller and Fornalutx.

Go through a gate (**2h25min**) and down some narrow stone steps, to come into **Binibassi**, a tiny hamlet of beautiful stone houses, where a water channel empties into a small trough. At the bottom of the steps, you will see a sign to 'Sóller' to the right. Follow this towards what appears to be a cul-de-sac. You will find that the path continues between the houses, passing a

35

Lunch on the terrace at Es Turó — beautiful, even in winter!

huge carob tree and some garage doors. It leads away from the houses of Binibassi between high stone walls. Keep winding down the valley and, at the bottom of more steps, go left down a wide track. At the bottom, take the first right turn, a tarmac road signposted to 'Sóller'. Follow this to the end, then turn left again, down to a main road. Turn right, walking beside a **stream bed** on your left. Go left over the **bridge (2h45min)** and keep straight ahead at each junction, rejoining **Carrer de Sa Lluna**. Turn right and, just a few metres along, you're back in the **Plaça de Sa Constitució**, with its many bars and cafés.

Es Turó

I've lost count of the times I have enjoyed a meal on the rustic, frond-green terrace of Es Turó. If you love mountain views and good food, here you have the perfect combination — overlooking the pretty village of Fornalutx, surrounded by high mountains and olive tree slopes, listening to the gentle water-music of mountain springs, and breathing in the heady perfume of orange blossoms in spring. It is, by the way, very popular with walkers.

They specialise in Mallorcan cuisine, and their particular presentation of the traditional *pa amb oli* is a meal in itself (see photograph on page 7): lashings of brown Mallorcan bread dripping with olive oil, fresh tomatoes, olives, cured ham, Mallorcan cheese, peppers, home-pickled capers and other goodies. In theory, a starter … but you won't be able to eat anything else! Reach perfection with a jug of local red wine.

Oven-baked cod at Es Turó

ES TURO
Avenida Arbona Colom Nº 6
07109 Fornalutx (971 630808
daily ex Thu and from 27 Dec to
5 Feb, lunch and dinner €

very varied menu, with plenty of **starters** to choose from; **salads, fish, meats**

specialities include *pa amb oli*, roast **suckling pig**, roast **lamb**, Mallorcan-style **codfish** bake, **spinach croquettes**, *sopas Mallorquinas* (Mallorcan vegetable soup), home-made **almond cake** and ice cream. Several of these recipes are described overleaf.

Ingredients (for 4 people)
1 bunch fresh spinach leaves
1 medium onion, chopped
2 cloves garlic, chopped
100 ml white sauce (2 tbsp
    olive oil to 4 tsp cornflour,
    then stir in enough milk to
    make a thick paste)
pine nuts to taste
salt and pepper
1 egg, lightly beaten
breadcrumbs to coat

Ingredients (for 4 people)
400 g salted cod (if not
    available, use frozen cod)
400 g potatoes, thinly sliced
vegetables to taste, all finely
    chopped and mixed: spring
    onions, leeks, Swiss chards,
    red pepper, garlic cloves
parsley, finely chopped (to
    garnish)
2 large tomatoes, sliced
50 g pine nuts
50 g seedless sultanas
ground black pepper
olive oil

Spinach croquettes (croquetes d'espinacs); not illustrated

Cook and drain the spinach, then chop up. Stir-fry the chopped onion and garlic, then mix with the white sauce, *using only enough white sauce to make a paste!* Add the pine nuts, spinach, salt & pepper. Mix together well; refrigerate for 24 hours.

Next day, beat in an egg, form into croquettes and roll in breadcrumbs. Deep fry and serve piping hot!

Oven-baked cod, Mallorcan-style (bacallà al forn); photo page 37

Soak the fish until ready for use. Chop into squares, and stir fry a bit. Fry the potatoes until translucent, and just sweat the vege-table mixture.

Pour a bit of olive oil into a *greixonera* (Mallorcan clay baking dish) and build up layers: potatoes at the bottom, then fish, then the vegetables (first mix in the pine nuts and sultanas). Top with more pota-toes, then the tomatoes. Sprinkle with ground black pepper, and dribble with olive oil. Bake at 220°C/425°F/gas mark 7 for 20-30min. Garnish with the parsley.

recipes

eat

Mallorcan dry vegetable soup *(sopas Mallorquinas)*

Pour some olive oil into a *greixonera* — the typical Mallorcan clay cooking pot (but a wok or large stir-fry pan will do), and stir-fry the chopped onions, spring onions, leeks and peppers until softened.

Later add the finely chopped tomatoes. Leave simmering on a low heat, and add the parsley, garlic cloves, cabbage, Swiss chard and cauliflower. Continue to simmer until the vegetables are just cooked but not soft; at this point they should just be covered by their own liquid (if not, add a little vegetable broth).

To serve, cover the base of each person's dish with a layer of wafer-thin brown Mallorcan bread *(sopas)*, and ladle the soup over them (with just enough broth to be soaked up by the bread), and the vegetables on top.

Now dribble some fresh olive oil over the top, add a squirt of lemon juice, a sprinkling of paprika, some grated lemon rind and parsley ... and a hot chilli if you like. Delicious!

Ingredients (for 4 people)
2 large onions, roughly chopped
1 bunch spring onions, chopped
3-4 large leeks, chopped
peppers (1 red, 1 green), chopped
parsley
several garlic cloves, whole
2 large tomatoes, skinned &
    finely chopped
1/2 green cabbage, finely chopped
1 bunch Swiss chards, finely
    chopped
1/2 cauliflower, in rosettes
olive oil
salt and paprika
sopas (wafer-thin slices of Mallorcan saltless bread, sold specially for this dish in bakeries)
1 lemon and its grated rind
chilli peppers (optional garnish)

One of the island's best walks, boasting both splendid views and historical interest. It takes in the best part of a circuit from Valldemossa along the famous 'Camí de S'Arxiduc'. You skirt the edge of a high plateau, then descend the island's northern cliffs — for a breathtaking approach to the picturesque mountain village of Deià.

camí de s'arxiduc

WALK

Ideally, you need to catch the early bus, allowing time for a coffee and a *coca de patata* (a sweet potato bun typical in Valldemossa) before setting off. You should be walking by around 9am in order to arrive at Deià in time for lunch.

Start the walk from the **bus stop** in **Valldemossa**: walk back up the main road towards Palma. Pass two large car parks, then go left up **Carrer de Na Más**. Take the first right (Carrer de Son Gual) towards the big house of **Son Gual**, but veer left just *before* the house. Take the next right fork, coming up to a high stone wall on Carrer Ametlers.

Distance: 11.5km/7.1mi; 4h30min

Grade: strenuous, with an ascent of about 550m/1800ft and a steep descent of about 650m/2130ft. You must be sure-footed and have a head for heights. *Not suitable in bad weather conditions, such as high winds or thick mists.*

Equipment: hiking boots, sunhat, water, snack, whistle, compass, windproof, extra clothing in winter

Transport: 🚌 L210 from Palma bus station to Valldemossa; return on the same line from Deià (several bus stops along the main road in Deià).

Refreshments en route:
cafés in Valldemossa for morning coffee
Restaurante Las Palmeras in Deià at the end of the walk

Points of interest:
the 'Camí de S'Arxiduc'

Turn left here, and then curve round to the right on **Carrer Ses Oliveres**. At the top you will find a stony path at the left of the high wire fence of a private drive. There is a small wooden **information hut** here, where a forestry ranger will tell you about routes open to the public. Parts of this area are currently closed for conservation work. The land (now called 'Vulture Mountain') has been taken over by a consortium of important local landowners and foundations protecting Mediterranean

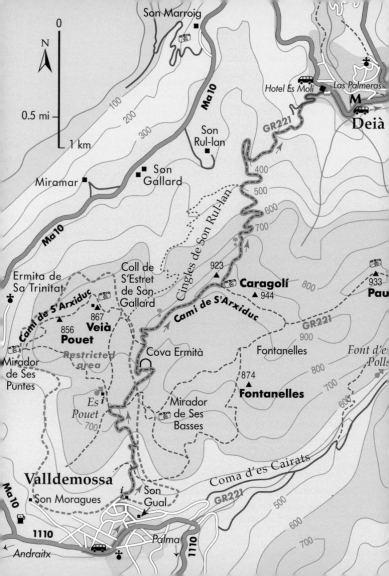

wildlife and black vultures. They are repairing years of damage done to the eco-system and hope to encourage black vultures to nest here again. *Please adhere to the restrictions; the rangers take their work seriously!*

Continue uphill for a few minutes, beside the fence, and turn left up a rocky path. A further five minutes along, having passed one or two disused woodcutters' trails, the route veers sharp right (red arrow) and follows a wide but stony woodcutters' trail that zigzags fairly steeply up through the woods. (A narrow earthen path up right, immediately past the ladder-stile, cuts off the first bend.)

Valldemossa — enjoy a *coca de patata* before you set off!

Rise to a **drystone wall** (**50min**) and go through the gateway. Just beyond the gateway you come onto level ground — an extensive shaded area, perfect for taking a breather.

Signposts here point to your ongoing route to the right: 'Camí Arxiduc, Deià'. (Not far ahead is a *sitja* and a clearing

43

Deià

with a well called Es Pouet. One hundred-plus visitors a day — over 300 a day on weekends — used to tramp past this spring, a key crossroads. The soil is as hard as concrete, the walls fallen down, and you can imagine the rubbish. So now Es Pouet lies within the dotted red line area on our map, and there is another rangers' checkpoint there to ensure walkers' compliance with the restrictions.

Heading right, begin to climb gently. Just three minutes up, you come to more signposts, including one for 'Cova Ermità, Camí Arxiduc, Deià', pointing you left along a newly built trail. Descend gently on an earthen path through the woods, passing a beautifully restored **lime kiln** (**1h**) on the left, as well as a low **drystone wall**, also restored. Past here the way heads to the right (same signs). An ascent begins, gentle at first, crossing a low stone wall and passing various *sitjas* — some double and even triple! Keep an eye out for **cairns**, some of them strategically placed on large rocks. After a while the route narrows into an earthen path and begins to climb in earnest, still in thick holm oak woods. As the path rises, the trees thin out, and stunning views open up over to the left as you cross rocky passes.

The 'Camí de S'Arxiduc' and the Archduke Luis Salvador

Luis Salvador was born in the Pitti Palace in Florence on 4th August 1847, son of Leopold II, Great Duke of Tuscany. But after his family's exile in 1859, most of his adolescence was spent in the Austro-Hungarian empire, where he studied law, philosophy and natural science.

As a young man he became interested in travelling, and he wrote his first travel book about Venice in 1868. He first came to Mallorca at the age of 20 with the idea of documenting the Balearics, but he never got further than Mallorca; it was love at first sight. He didn't return until 1871, and from then onwards he stayed, buying up huge properties and restoring old Mallorcan mansions, helping to build roads and hostels (where travellers were allowed free accommodation). All of his houses were open to the public; he even wrote guides to some of them.

He was also a keen rider. The **Camí de S'Arxiduc**, the archduke's bridlepath, was one of his major undertakings. This stone-laid trail, which we hikers enjoy so much, was built purely for his riding pleasure. It originally ran from Valldemossa up onto the high plateau, from where Luis Salvador could admire many of his properties below — Son Moragues, Miramar, Son Galceran, Son Gallard, Son Marroig, Sa Pedrissa... Many of these houses are now museums, containing the original furniture, documents, books and seafaring equipment belonging to the archduke.

On Puig Caragolí (944m), just beyond the turn-off to Cingles de Son Rul-lan, there is a plaque dedicated to the Archduke Luis Salvador on behalf of all Mallorcan mountaineers.

Eventually, at the top of a long slope, you come upon a **huge boulder with a cairn** on top (**1h30min**). Just beyond it there's a stone-walled enclosure and the **Cova Ermità** (Hermit's Cave) on the right — a fascinating place. It's big! There are a couple of rooms with windows, a fireplace, beds and even books. One can spend the night here — if it's not already 'bagged' ...

From the cave continue straight ahead along the now walled-in and stonier path and, quickly joining the ancient **Camí de S'Arxiduc**, zigzag steeply up to the high plateau. The views are magnificent! To the west, Galatzó thrusts its peak through scudding clouds, and the high pine-covered mountains of Planici rise up from the valley; below you lies Sa Foradada on a long stretch of rugged coastline; to the south, Palma's huge round bay glistens like a mirror, bordered by the high cliffs of Cap Blanc, with the isle of Cabrera on a hazy horizon. But this stone-laid trail skirts the edge of a high plateau, with very precipitous drops to the left; be *extra vigilant* along here if it happens to be misty or windy!

Eventually (**2h20min**) two **large cairns** mark your descent down the **Cingles de Son Rul-lan**; veer left, off the Archduke's Way, to follow the cairn-marked route (GR221) down the slopes towards what looks like the edge of the cliff. Look carefully for the small cleft where the path continues its descent, hugging the face of the cliff, and coming into trees lower down. About 50 minutes down from the top, the path goes sharp right, to pass a well-preserved stone-built **bread oven** and cross a *sitja*. Go through a gap in a wall and rise to a wider trail, with open views over Deià. The trail makes a U-turn to the right just before some rusty gates near **Son Rul-lan**.

Still following the cairns, you descend ancient cobbles and then a narrow zigzag path. At a track just below a farmhouse, turn right to descend past the beautiful **Hotel Es Molí** and emerge on the Ma-10 in Deià (**4h30min**). Turn right, to rise into **Deià village**, where you'll find **Las Palmeras** restaurant.

Las Palmeras

There are many restaurants and terraces with lovely views in Deià, but I always end up at 'Las Palmeras' — they are so welcoming!

LAS PALMERAS
C/ Arxiduc Lluis Salvador 11
07179 Deià (971 639016
**daily ex Wed (and winter evenings)
for lunch and dinner €€**

great variety of **starters**, including **paella**, **fish soup**, **escudella** (vegetable soup), **trempó** (a basic salad of mild onions, tomatoes, sweet peppers and olive oil, with various additions according to taste — like tuna), **tumbet** (recipes on pages 80, 112), **squids** in sauce, **duck confit**, **croquettes**, **sobrasada** (cured pork sausage), **patés** and hot **peppers**

fresh fish daily

meat dishes include lamb chops, fillet steak, and cabbage stuffed with pork

desserts feature **mandarin sorbet**, creme caramel, apple sorbet with calvados, **almond cake** and **almond ice cream**

The terrace of Las Palmeras

The cuisine is mostly Mallorcan, but they also do Spanish *tapas* and paella and offer a taste of Italy with **vegetarian** *tallarines* (tagliatelli). They are happy to prepare you meals to take away, but take-aways must be ordered 24 hours in advance. Tip: their freshly made garlic mayonnaise is wonderful!

restaurants

eat

Stuffed aubergines *(alberginies farcides)*

Boil the aubergines until softish, then cut in half lengthwise and empty out the pulp. In a frying pan, stir-fry the minced meat in a little olive oil, add the salt, oregano and pepper, and put into a mixing

bowl. Blend in the beaten egg, together with the aubergine pulp, and some freshly chopped parsley. Place the empty halves on a baking tray, and fill with the mixture. Bake in a moderate oven (180°C/350°F/gas mark 4) for 20min.

To make the sauce, stir-fry the tomatoes with the chopped onion and crushed garlic. Add the bay leaf and let simmer to a thick lumpy sauce. Pour over the baked aubergines before serving.

Ingredients (for 4 people)

2 large aubergines
400 g minced meat (usually beef, but any kind)
parsley and oregano
salt and pepper
1 egg, beaten
olive oil

For the sauce

6 large tomatoes, skinned and finely chopped
1 clove garlic, crushed
1 onion, chopped
bay leaf

Stuffed apricots, avocados or custard apples (for 4 people)

Menus can change with a change of chef. This dish is no longer on offer at Palmeras, but why not make it anyway?

Halve 2 large fruits and take out the stones. Mix together the following ingredients: 1 tin of flaked tuna fish, mayonnaise, finely chopped spring onions, fresh (or dried) basil. Fill the fruit with the mixture and serve chilled.

Almond cake and ice cream
(gató/gelat d'ametla)

First make the ice cream. Put all the ingredients in a saucepan and bring to the boil, stirring all the time. Let simmer 1-2min, still stirring, then pour into a flat aluminium or plastic container. Let it cool, stirring occasionally.

Remove the cinnamon and lemon rind and put the container in the freezer. For a smoother result, stir from time to time as it freezes, to disperse the crystals.

In the meantime, preheat the oven to 180°C/350°F/gas mark 4. Grease a 25 cm/9 in loose-bottomed cake tin with butter and dust with caster sugar, shaking out the excess.

Beat together the sugar and egg yolks until the mixture is very frothy. Separately, beat the egg whites until stiff. Add the ground almonds, lemon rind and cinnamon to the yolk/sugar mixture; stir. Finally, fold in the egg whites.

Spoon into the tin (it should come 3/4 way to the top) and bake for 30-40min — or until a toothpick inserted into the middle comes out clean. Cool and sprinkle with caster sugar to serve.

Ingredients (12-14 servings)

For the cake:

600 g finely ground almonds
500 g caster sugar
9 eggs, separated
1 lemon rind, grated
1 tsp ground cinnamon
knob of butter

For the ice cream:

1 l milk _(or water)_
250 g finely ground almonds
 (raw or roasted)
300 g caster sugar
rind of 1 lemon, _not_ grated
1 or 2 stick(s) cinnamon

recipes

eat

Bunyola lies in the foothills below the long limestone Serra d'Alfábia. These hills are covered with some of the most beautiful and unspoilt pine forests left on Mallorca. Penyal d'Honor (809m) is a magnificent viewpoint from which to admire the Orient Valley, the Alfábia Ridge, and fold upon fold of dense surrounding woodlands.

around bunyola
WALK

Start the walk from **Bunyola railway station** by going right, up **Costa de s'Estació** (Station Hill) into the village. Follow the main road as it bends sharp right, to pass the village square and **church**, then cross over and go left up **Carrer Mare de Deu de la Neu**. At the top of this road turn right along **Carrer Santa Catalina Thomàs**, and shortly take the second, sharp left turn up **Carrer d'Orient**. Follow the wide steps as far as the **drinking fountain**, where you can fill your water bottles.

Go right directly opposite the fountain, up the twisting stone stairway, signposted 'Sa Comuna d'es Grau'. You wind steeply up between the little houses. Higher up, look back for a lovely view down over Bunyola. Continue up to the top, then carry on along a wide track. Up ahead you can see some big caves in the hillside. Just as the track begins to descend to the right, veer left between drystone walls (same signposting), into the woods (**25min**).

Distance: 14km/8.7mi; 4h30min

Grade: strenuous, with an ascent of some 570m/1870ft and descent of 600m/1970ft

Equipment: walking boots, water, snack, **torch**, suncream, warm clothing in winter

Transport: 🚌 L211 or 🚂 to Bunyola (Sóller line, see pages 21 and 137). You need to take the 08.00 train from Palma in order to complete the walk in time for lunch. Or, if you want to make a day of it, you could start later, do a leisurely walk with a picnic en route, and finish the walk with an evening meal at the restaurant.

Refreshments en route:
cafés in Bunyola for morning coffee
La Terraza de Bunyola restaurant at the end of the walk

Points of interest:
Ca's Garriguer refuge and picnic area. It is possible to hire the stone-built refuge to sleep overnight; telephone Bunyola town hall at (971 613007 or 148201 for permission.
Cova de l'Amo Guillem (where you'll use your torch)

The path climbs between pine trees, pampas grass, rock roses and tree heather, and soon you come up to an old **limekiln**. Continue uphill to the right, and a little higher you pass the remains of an *aljub* (an Arab water deposit construction covered by a drystone arch), half of it still intact after a thousand years. A few minutes later, the route narrows and bends to the right, becoming a steep, stone-laid trail — part of the original centuries-old route up to Es Grau, restored in 1990, for which we walkers are very grateful. It climbs higher and higher, zigzagging up the side of the cliff, and eventually begins to level out onto an earthen path, with superb views over left towards the Teix and Galera mountains.

Soon the path drops down onto a wider track (**1h10min**), where a one-minute detour down to the left will bring you to the **'mirador'** — a high viewpoint on the edge of the escarpment, from where you have an excellent panorama (*take extreme care near the edge*). Continue uphill to the right, climbing more gently between the trees, until you meet a wider track coming in from below and to the right (**1h20min**). Follow the signpost pointing left, to 'Ca's Garriguer'. Suddenly you feel you are being swallowed up by the forest. The wide stony track, covered in dark green moss, is deep in shadow, the tall trees and heavy foliage scarcely allowing any daylight to penetrate, and all is enveloped in a deep and solemn silence — it is beautiful.

You pass one or two **limekilns** and come to a signposted 'crossroads' (**1h35min**); uphill to the right is a direct route to the refuge of Ca's Garriguer; left is a cul-de-sac. Your route lies straight ahead, up the signposted **Comellar d'en Cupì**. You pass a couple of *sitjas* (circular earthen mounds where charcoal was once burned) and climb up the narrow gully *(comellar)*, soon rising to a wide track. Veer left to join it, and turn left to follow this track for another 25 minutes as it continues to climb gently over the hills.

Keep a sharp lookout for the **wooden signpost** to 'Penyal d'Honor'; it's on a tree to the left, just where the **main track dips before rising**

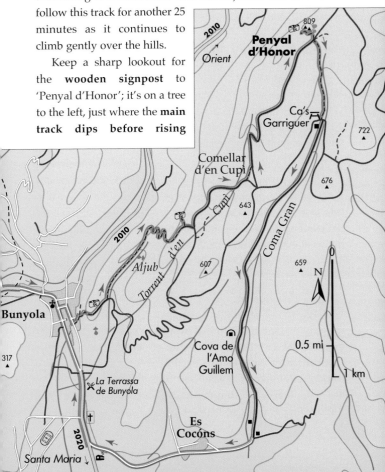

Almond orchards on the way back to Bunyola

sharply (**2h10min**). Go left up this narrow, cairned path; in 10 minutes you will reach the double peak of the lower of the two 'Penyals', **Penyal d'Honor** (809m; **2h20min**). One of the peaks holds a fenced-off fire vigilance post, so *(using extreme care!)* climb the rocks up to the right-hand peak for a bird's eye view! The high Serra d'Alfábia with its meteorological and TV paraphernalia stretches away in front of you, and you now see Bunyola in miniature, nestling far below to the southwest against the backcloth of the high Teix ridge and craggy lower foothills, with the triangular peak of L'Ofre to the northeast. The dense pine forests stretch away in the east like a green cloth draped over the contours, with the escarpments of Puig d'Alaró and its castle on the horizon. On the southern skyline the wide bay of Palma glistens in the sun.

Descend back to the track and cross over, to take the **narrow path almost directly opposite** (slightly left, but *not* the wide curving path); your path is marked with cairns. This drops steeply through the woods and widens out further down, becoming a very pleasant woodland walk. You meet the main track at **Ca's Garriguer**, where it curves round the picnic area

(**2h45min**). Keep left, ignoring the gated-off track, and walk down to the well and refuge.

Keep on the stony track and descend through a wide gateway, to continue winding down through these lovely quiet woodlands. After you go through a **gate** (**3h30min**), you suddenly emerge from the tree line onto open olive tree terraces. A rough track takes you between drystone walls, and later the olives give way to almond orchards. Beyond another gate, you descend a narrow gorge and come to the curious **Cova de l'Amo Guillem** on the right-hand side of the track (**3h45min**).

Cova de l'Amo Guillem (Master William's cave)
This cave-house sits underneath an enormous overhang, very reminiscent of the cave houses at Cosconas near Lluc. The door is usually open — hikers often use it to sleep in — and with your torch you can explore the big cave at the back. (I'd advise you, however, not to linger below the rotted beams just inside the entrance.) By the side of the house there is a big fireplace under the charcoal-blackened rocky overhang, and some rudimentary walled 'rooms' with ruined water catchments. To the left of the house, a deep well hides behind another (new) wooden door. It is certainly an interesting place!

Further down the track, go through a rickety **gate by a small house** (**4h**) and pass a second house on a corner. Continue ahead, ignoring a track off left. Follow this rough tarmac lane all the way back to the **electricity plant** on the Bunyola/Santa Maria road (**4h20min**). Turn right and walk past the **cemetery**. A couple of minutes will bring you to **La Terraza de Bunyola** (just before the village, on the right; **4h30min**). Then walk back to the station.

La Terraza de Bunyola

This rustic country place is very popular with walkers, either because it happens to be at the end of a fabulous walk or because the cooking is so good — probably both. It's also very economical,

so you can't go wrong! It changed hands since the last edition of this book and is now an Italian restaurant specialising in fresh home-made pastas and pizzas. The chef, Alberto Mancini, and his sous-chef Dino are both Italian.

They offer a **menu del día** priced at 10 € — a three-course meal with a choice between various starters and main

LA TERRAZA DE BUNYOLA
Carretera de Bunyola–Santa Maria, km0,6 (971 615039
closed November, otherwise open daily from 13.00-15.30 and from 19.30 until 23.30 €-€€

starter salads are really special – like tomato, mozzarella and gambas; tuna tartare or carpaccio with vitello; antipasto, burrata with serrano ham

grilled **fish** and **seafood**

meats: steaks, lamb chops and pork escalopes with various sauces or mushrooms

specialities: **fresh home-made pastas** (tagliatelli with shrimps, mushrooms or vegetables; tortelli with bolognese or cream sauce and ham; gnocci with pesto, au gratin, mushrooms)

risottos with seafood or gorgonzola and spinach

wide range of crispy-based **pizzas** (take-away service too)

home-made tiramisu and **pannecotta**

restaurants

eat

courses, with dessert and drink, as well as a 'chefs suggestion menu' which changes every 15 days. The wine list is more than adequate.

Depending on the weather, you can sit inside the glassed-in lower terrace, the cosier interior, or up on the elevated outdoor terrace under the trees.

Mallorcan ratatouille *(tumbet)*

This recipe dates from La Terraza's previous incarnation, when it featured Mallorcan cuisine.

Fry the potatoes in oil until they just start to turn brown, then set aside. In a large *greixonera* (Mallorcan clay pot) stir-fry the onion until transparent, then add the peppers, aubergines, marrow, herbs and garlic cloves, and stir-fry gently for about 10min.

Add the tomatoes, then the potatoes and vegetable stock, and simmer for a further 10min or so. Serve hot with *pan moreno* (Mallorcan brown bread).

Ingredients (for 4 people)

2 large aubergines, chopped
2 red peppers and 2 green peppers, cut into large pieces
1 large onion, cut in rings
1 courgette (2 if small), sliced
2 or 3 potatoes, peeled and finely sliced
3 or 4 tomatoes, skins on, but chopped
olive oil
garlic cloves, whole, to taste
salt & pepper
basil, thyme, oregano
1 cup vegetable broth or stock

recipes

eat

The once-magnificent Castell d'Alaró was so impregnable a fortress that an Arab commander was able to hold out for almost two years after the Reconquest of Mallorca by Jaime I in 1229. Much of its old wall still stands defiant, blending reluctantly with the sheer reddish escarpments, thousands of feet above the plain.

castell d'alaró

WALK

Start the walk at **km11.9 on the Alaró/Orient road**, opposite the farm of **Son Bernadàs** (selling fresh produce, honey, home-made *herbes* and cold-pressed olive oil — if you bring your own bottle).

Facing Orient, go up through the access gate on the left and veer left round a large **water tank**, to walk through terraces planted with olive trees. In **3min** you'll see 'Castillo' painted on a rock at ground level; keep ahead. After **10min** the path begins its steep zigzag climb through the woods. At **30min** you will come to a **grassy outcrop** at the right of the path — an excellent vantage point from which to photograph the Orient Valley. A little further up, go through an old gateway, giving access to a little clearing. The path continues up to the right, and comes up to a wide track (**40min**). Turn up right here and, almost immediately, you will find yourself in a large clearing on the col known as **Es Pouet** (**45min**). You may be surprised to see cars parked here! It is possible to drive up from Alaró on the other side of the

Distance: 11km/6.8mi; 4h30min

Grade: easy-moderate, with some steepish slopes near the start. Gentle ascent of some 330m/1080ft; descent of some 560m/1850ft

Equipment: hiking boots, water, sunhat, suncream, warm clothing in winter, **rope** (see page 63)

Transport: Inca 🚆 to Consell, 🚌 L320 to Alaró, then taxi ((971 518308 or 696 467318) to Orient — ask to alight at 'Son Bernadás'. (Note: the Alaró taxi can also be found by going to the 'Cibercafé Alaró' at the top of the main road, on the right-hand corner; see map overleaf.)

Refreshments: bar/restaurant at the hikers' lodge on the Puig d'Alaró summit; Restaurante 'Es Vergé' on the descent, 45min below the summit

Points of interest:
Son Bernadàs farm
ruins of Alaró Castle

The trail up to Alaró Castle

mountain, but is not recommended for hired cars or nervous motorists! You may also come across some donkeys, the amiable transport 'vehicles' waiting to be laden with provisions when the jeep arrives from a shopping trip down on the plain. They appreciate a pat on the muzzle.

Cross this clearing to the stone wall at the top and find the beginning of the centuries-old **stone-laid trail** on your left (signposted). Soon the awesome escarpments of the **Puig d'Alaró** loom up ahead, as the trail becomes a series of stone steps winding ever higher towards the top. In **1h10min** go through the imposing archways and the entrance to the **Castell d'Alaró**, to come onto a flatter, grassy, wooded area, from where the views are superb. On the left lies the incredibly beautiful and unspoilt valley of Sollerich, with its backcloth of high mountains, the peaks of

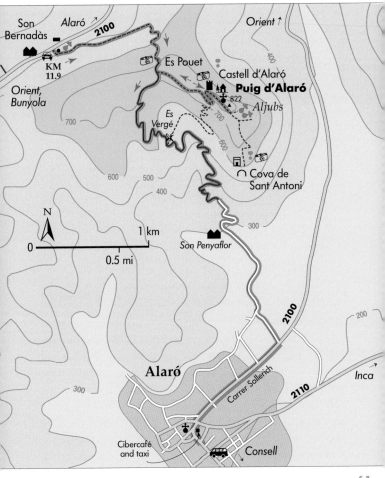

Son Bernadàs

Alaró ↗

2100

KM 11.9

Orient, Bunyola

Es Pouet

Orient ↑

400

Castell d'Alaró

Puig d'Alaró

822 ▲

Aljubs

Es Vergé

700

600

500

400

700

⌒ Cova de Sant Antoni

N

1 km

0

0.5 mi

300

Son Penyaflor

300

2100

200

Alaró

Carrer Sollerich

2110

Inca →

300

Cibercafé and taxi

Consell

Arriving through the imposing entrance to the Castell d'Alaró

L'Ofre and Massanella, and many others. To the right, the wide sweep of the plain reaches down as far as Palma and its huge circular bay. *Extra care* is needed near the unprotected precipitous drop on the left! It is wiser to admire the view to the north from a little further uphill, where there is a protecting wall. Then continue up to the **hikers' lodge** (where you could have a meal or stay overnight; see page 66) and the little pilgrims' **chapel** (**1h20min**).

Intrepid, sure-footed walkers may like to enquire at the

lodge whether access to the Cova de Sant Antoni and/or the Arab water tanks shown on page 64 is permitted. These paths are shown on the map, but not highlighted in colour . Nor are the routes described, since the land has been closed off by the owners. (Alaró town council have been trying to persuade them to reinstate access for walkers, but without success as of press date.) If access *is* possible, the cairned diversion to the cave, which passes an old watchtower, will take about an hour (times are *not* included in the main walk times). *Do not enter the cave without a torch and a rope* (there is an iron rope-hold at the entrance). If

you don't have a head for heights, and prefer safer walking, just visit the Arab water tanks *(aljubs)* if access is possible: go through the metal gate by the latrines, and fork left in about three minutes. Another few minutes down and you're there. Take care at the steep drop beyond the lowest tank.

The return route leaves the castle ruins via the stone steps*, which you take back down to the large clearing of Es Pouet

---

*If you decided to eat at the hikers' lodge, halfway down the steps, on a bend, you could take the trail straight ahead signposted to 'Alaró'. This will bring you out *below* the Es Vergé restaurant. This shortens the descent a little.

Aljub (Arab water tank) on Puig d'Alaró, shown below

(**1h40min**). Bear left here, to follow the wide track down the hill. The track zigzags down the slopes, and makes for pleasant walking, with beautiful far-reaching views across the plain.

When you arrive at the houses of **Es Vergé** (**2h05min**), you will see a recently enlarged car park for those who dare to drive up. The oven-roast lamb at this restaurant (which, confusingly, is called 'Es Pouet' by some local people) is so good that people come from all over the island. So unless you booked, you may or may not be lucky enough to get a table!

Well-fed, and raring to go again, it's easy now to descend to Alaró. Just continue down the track from the restaurant, still high above the plain, and be sure to look out for the short cuts: they are all cairn-marked and are the remnants of the old trail which was interrupted by the newer

View from the castle down to Es Vergé and the onward track towards Alaró

track. The trail leads down through beautiful olive tree terraces and rejoins the main track from time to time.

Further down you pass the rural hotel of **Son Penyaflor**, once a Mallorcan country estate. Take the first left turn (**4h15min**), to come down to the Alaró/Orient road (Ma2100). Turn right here, to enter the village of **Alaró** (**4h30min**). The bus stop is at No 2, Joan Alcover, just around the corner from the Avinguda de la Constitució, the main through road.

Castell d'Alaró hikers' lodge

These ruins, once a Moorish stronghold, rebuilt after the Reconquest of Mallorca in 1229 by King Jaume I of Aragon, are all that is left of an impregnable fortress and citadel that once covered the entire top of this mountain, with only one access route: an ancient cobbled trail up a steep cliff. The entrance and ruins are still very impressive, however, towering above the plain at over 800m.

Bar-tavern near the hikers' lodge and chapel

Rooms are on offer to the weary traveller at the **hikers' lodge** on the highest point, where you can also enjoy a meal. It costs 12 € per adult to spent a night in the dormitory on bunk-beds (15,50 € B&B, 24 € half-board), and the refuge is open all year round. Facilities include a living room with fireplace, showers, heating and hot water. There is also a small cosy bar-tavern at the right of the chapel, where you can get *pa amb oli*, Mallorcan pastries and hot or cold drinks — from 09.00-23.00.

CASTELL D'ALARO HIKERS' LODGE
(971 940 503 or 971 182 112 or email reserves@castellalaro.cat for information or to book.
open daily all year round €
www.castellalaro.cat (in English)

bar-tavern and **restaurant** serving *very* simple meals: at press date cod paella or roast lamb for lunch, sausage and chips or a vegetarian dish for supper.

restaurants

eat

Es Vergé

Without a doubt the 'Aladdin's cave' of restaurants — full of culinary (and other) treasures! Push open the old wooden door to walk into a small dining area by the huge fireplace, and either

RESTAURANTE ES VERGE
Camí d'es Castell ℂ 971 182126
open every day of the year €

Mallorcan dishes: **snails** with garlic mayonnaise, **arròs brut** (see page 93), **frito Mallorquín** (see page 81), **sopas Mallorquinas** (see page 39)

fish dishes might be oven-baked **cod** with peppers and tomatoes, grilled **squid**, or grilled **prawns**

for **meat** there is roast **suckling pig**, **roast lamb**, lamb chops, pork chops

desserts are special! — strawberry cake, walnut and custard tart, apple pie, almond cake, cheesecake, and of course, ice creams

Hungry hikers tucking in at Es Vergé, downstairs by the fireplace

Antonia or Francisca will usher you to a table. If the room looks full, not to worry — two large dining rooms hide at the top of the staircase (with its original handrail of cartwheels). There is also another smaller room below.

The centuries-old stone oven at the back is the secret of the best roast lamb you have ever tasted (plus of course the equally secret ingredients that go to make up the broth in which they bake it!). The lamb roasts all morning, while you are hard at work on the mountain trails. Their menu, however, is very varied; you can get anything from a sandwich (*bocadillo*) or salad to the dishes listed in the mini-menu.

Roast meat marinade

Here's how to achieve really tender joints of oven-roast meat — pork, lamb, kid, whatever. Mix together in a blender 100 ml olive

Lamb roasting at Es Vergé (above) and ready to serve (left)

oil, 100 ml brandy, 200 ml water, 50 ml freshly squeezed lemon juice and 2-3 garlic cloves — you should obtain a creamy liquid. Marinate the meat in the liquid (enough to cover) overnight. The next day slow roast in the oven in about an inch of the same mixture, basting occasionally, until tender.

The late *Madó* Maria, who ran the Son Bernadàs farm with her husband Tomeu, used an old Mallorcan recipe book printed in Felanitx in the late 1800s, adding her own personal touch to each dish — she gave me the next two recipes.

Baked shark steaks *(mussola)*

The *tintorera* (called *mussola* in Mallorcan supermarkets) is a Mediterranean shark — its white

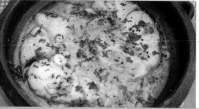

Ingredients (for 4 people)
4 shark steaks
large bunch of of spring onions, finely chopped
3 tbsp chopped parsley
olive oil
juice of 1 lemon
1 tsp cornflour
100 ml milk
fresh basil to taste
salt & pepper

meat is delicious! (Back home, you can try this recipe with tuna or swordfish steaks.)

Gently fry the steaks in a little olive oil, adding the lemon juice, salt and pepper. Lift out onto a plate and set aside. In a *greixonera* (clay cooking vessel) stir-fry the spring onions and the parsley, add a teaspoon of cornflour, and stir in the milk. Place the pieces of fish on top and sprinkle with fresh basil. Bake at 180°C/350°F/gas mark 4 for 10min. Maria sometimes tops the fish with slices of tomato.

Rabbit and onions
(conill amb seba)

Chop the rabbit into smallish pieces. Cover the base of a *greixonera* with olive oil and stir-fry the *sobrasada* until it has deposited its colour and some flavouring in the pot, then discard.

Stir-fry the well-seasoned rabbit pieces until golden brown, add the bacon pieces, and after a couple of minutes add the onions. Continue to stir-fry on a low heat until the onions brown.

Add the wine, stock and bay leaf, and simmer slowly until the rabbit is tender. Sprinkle over the cinnamon and serve with *pan moreno* (Mallorcan brown bread).

Ingredients (for 4 people)
large rabbit or hare (preferably wild)
100 g thick bacon, chopped
a small piece of *sobrasada*
   (Mallorcan sausage)
3 large onions, finely chopped
150 ml white wine
150 ml stock
olive oil
salt & pepper
1 bay leaf
1/2 tsp cinnamon

recipes

eat

This lovely walk starts from the magical mountain village of Orient, set in a green and fertile valley untouched as yet by mass tourism, although frequently visited by hikers. Why not climb the stone steps up to the quiet little square by the churchyard before beginning your walk today? It's very picturesque.

orient to santa maria

WALK

Start out at **Orient**: walk along the quiet country lane towards 'Bunyola' for just over **20min**, then turn left down a wide earthen track (the second one you come to, just where the road begins to climb in bends). Go over the wooden **ladder-stile** and continue along a walled-in track. Climb another **ladder-stile** over a gate (**35min**), and cross the stream bed further down — on stepping stones if water is flowing — to find some **wooden signposts** on the left.

Before continuing up the opposite slope, make a short descent to see one of Mallorca's impressive (if it has rained recently) waterfalls — the Salt d'es Freu. To get there, go straight down the wide walled-in path at the left of the stream bed. This descends in long zigzags for about 10 minutes and, just where it

Distance: 14.5km/9mi; 5h

Grade: easy, with a short ascent of about 160m/525ft; otherwise gentle descents (down a tarmac lane for the last 1h30min)

Equipment: hiking boots, long-sleeved shirt, trousers, insect repellent, sunhat, suncream, water, whistle, **torch**, warm clothing in winter

Transport: 🚆 from Palma to Consell, 🚌 L320 to Alaró, then taxi (see Walk 4, page 59) to Orient village; return by 🚆 from Santa Maria (every 30min)

Refreshments en route:
Ca'n Jaume in Orient
Celler Sa Sini in Santa Maria

Points of interest:
Salt d'es Freu waterfall
Avenc de Son Pou (cave); **see important notes on page 77**

Note: If you do this walk in reverse, you might like to spend a night in Orient. I recommend the hotel Dalt Muntanya, C/ Bunyola-Orient km10, 07349 Orient. (971 148283/fax 971 615373; www.daltmuntanya.net; e-mail: info@daltmuntanya.net. This cosy country hotel offers luxury in each of its 18 differently decorated rooms, plus an unforgettable evening meal in the restaurant or outside on the terrace.

passes between rock walls (on a bend to the right), you come to the high cascade of the **Salt d'es Freu (45min)**, where the rushing waters of the Freu stream tumble noisily down over the rocks — very impressive when flowing, but also beautiful in dry weather, when you can explore (*carefully!*) over the huge green moss-covered boulders.

Back up at the signposts, begin to zigzag to the right up the hillside and, at the top, continue straight ahead. When you come to an **arrow marker (1h20min)** turn sharp right as indicated, cross a *sitja* (earthen mound where charcoal was once burned), pass a **limekiln**, and continue ahead, gently descending. Some 25 minutes lower down, the **path narrows quite a bit**, and runs high above the east

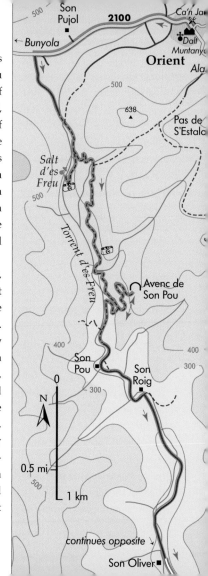

continues opposite →

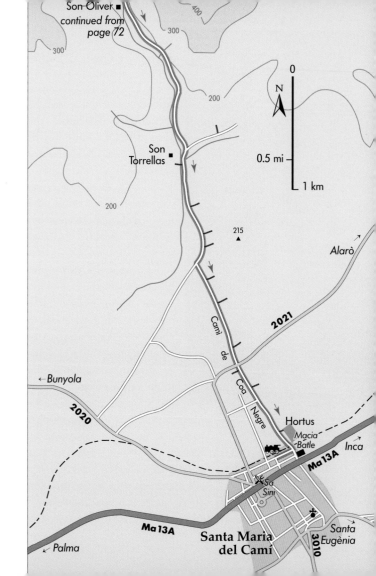

Son Oliver ■

continued from page 72

400

300

300

200

N

Son
Torrellas ■

0.5 mi

1 km

215 ▲

Alaró →

Camí   de

2021

← Bunyola

2020

Coa

Negre

Hortus

Macia
Batle ■

Inca →

Ma 13A

Sa
Sini

← Palma

Ma 13A

Santa Maria
del Camí

Santa
Eugènia

3010

Salt d'es Freu
This is one of Mallorca's most visited waterfalls, mainly because it is easy to reach from the Orient/Bunyola road. A truly beautiful cascade after heavy rains, many visit just to photograph it!

bank of the gorge, where the **Torrent d'es Freu** flows through a wild and beautiful landscape. Continue over a **rocky pass (1h50min)**, the ideal place for a drink stop or a snack, perched up on the karst rocks under the shade of pines, high above the gorge, with lovely views down over the torrent as it travels south between thickly wooded slopes.

After this, the rocky path descends abruptly, delving deeper into the woods. A few minutes lower down the path appears to end, but you can climb up left onto a wall-supported path above the stone wall. Soon you come to the turn-off left uphill to the Avenc de Son Pou, a narrow earthen path just by some **signposts** to 'Orient' and 'Santa Maria'. It is a steep climb up to the gated entrance inside the long rock tunnel access to the **Avenc de Son Pou (2h20min)**.

Orient, backed by the Serra d'Alfabia

After exploring the cave (see overleaf), return to the main path and keep descending, coming down to stream bed level and then walking along the eastern bank of the stream, eventually coming onto a track. Some 50m/yds before the track ends, go left over some rocks and through an **access gate** by the side of the houses of **Son Pou**, to return to the track. Keeping straight ahead now, you come onto tarmac by the houses of **Son Oliver (3h40min)**.

Continue south for some 3km, then fork left down **Camí de Coa Negre**. At **Santa Maria** you come to the railway crossing

Avenc de Son Pou

At the time of writing, these wonderful caverns can only be visited on Sundays, but it is worth contacting the Santa Maria town hall Mon-Fri *only* (℃ 971 620131/fax 971 140337), as visiting days tend to change. The barred metal gate inside the access tunnel was put there some years ago to protect the caves from vandalism and stalactite thieving. This is opened for visitors with an appointment; however, there is a small access at the bottom big enough to crawl through.

If you are lucky enough to be able to visit, you can explore the immense cavities of these underground halls; the main one is over 50m high and has a hole in the roof allowing daylight to flood in, an amazing phenomenon around midday! Some steps lead down to a smaller grotto, which is much dimmer, while the third chamber is in utter darkness. With the help of your torch you can admire the various formations and the enormous stalactites and stalagmites.

and **railway station**, just by the Hortus Garden Centre and Macià Batle bodega (**5h**). To find Sa Sini, continue ahead to the main Inca/Palma road and turn right, into the village centre. When you come to the 'Bunyola' turn-off on the right, just there on the corner is the **Celler Sa Sini**, ready to welcome you!

Ca'n Jaume

This restaurant reputedly serves the best roast suckling pig on the island! If you do this walk in reverse, you could try it.

Otherwise, the delightful terrace overlooking the Serra d'Alfàbia is perfect for morning coffee, or why not try a Mallorcan *berenar* (snack) for breakfast — *frito Mallorquin, pa amb oli* ... before you start?

'Celler' restaurant Ca'n Jaume

RESTAURANTE CA'N JAUME
Carretera Alaró–Bunyola s/n, Orient (971 615153
closed Tuesdays, otherwise open for drinks and snacks from 09.00; for meals from 13.00-15.30/16.00, 20.00-23.00 €€

starters include Mallorcan specialities like **arròs brut, sopas Mallorquinas, frits, snails** and croquettes, as well as a variety of salads

meat dishes like **roast suckling pig**, roast lamb, pork and lamb chops

desserts feature **gató d'ametla** (recipe page 49), ice creams, chocolate cake, fresh fruit, etc

restaurants
eat

Celler Sa Sini

Old pictures, Mallorcan pottery, clocks and other *objets d'art* decorate the colourful walls and columns of Sa Sini, where, as well as good food, you'll enjoy the congenial atmosphere of a typical Mallorcan *celler* restaurant. It is very popular with the locals. The desserts are especially good — just look at the selection in the photograph!

CELLER SA SINI
Plaça Hostals 20, Santa Maria (971 620252
closed Mondays, otherwise open from 13.00-16.00 and 20.00-23.30 (24.00 in summer €€

specialities are Mallorcan dishes: ***arròs brut, sopas Mallorquinas, frito Mallorquín, frit de matances, snails, rabbit and onion***

various **fish** and **meat** dishes

20 different home-made **pizzas**

vegetarian offerings include **lasagne** (recipe overleaf), pizzas, **pasta** with mushrooms, etc

good **desserts**, among them apple pie, cheesecake with cranberries, almond cake, ice creams

Sa Sini (above) and the dining room at Dalt Muntanya in Orient (see page 71)

Vegetarian lasagne *(lasagne vegetal)*

Stir-fry the chopped onion and leeks in a little olive oil with some salt and pepper and the oregano. Add the mushrooms and the broccoli florets and stir-fry a couple of minutes.

In an oven dish, put some of the mixture in the base, add a sheet of pasta and cover with white sauce; repeat the operation until the dish is full. Top with white sauce and a good layer of cheese. Dribble a little olive oil over the top, and bake in a moderate oven (180°C/350°F/gas mark 4) for 20-30min, then grill until the cheese covering browns.

In case you're not familiar with Havarti cheese, it takes its name from the Danish experimental farm where it was developed. It's a semi-soft pale yellow cheese similar to tilsit. If you can't get Havarti, use cheddar or any cheese that grills well.

<u>Ingredients (for 4 people)</u>

12 lasagne sheets
2 bunches of broccoli, in florets
1 kg chopped mushrooms
2 leeks, chopped
1 small onion, chopped
250 ml white sauce (see page 38)
1 tsp oregano
salt & pepper
olive oil
4 Havarti cheese slices

recipes

eat

Here are two typical Mallorcan 'starters' recipes. The packages of mixed seafood sold at M&S and some supermarkets are ideal if you are making the *frit mariner* back home.

Seafood stir-fry (frit mariner); not illustrated

Fry the potatoes in a little olive oil until soft, then set aside. Stir fry the peppers with the salt and pepper for about 3min. Then add the seafood, garlic and fennel and stir-fry till warmed through. Add the peas, and finally the potatoes, and stir-fry all together for a couple of minutes.

Frito Mallorquín

First fry the potato until cooked, then set aside. Then, in a *greixonera* (Mallorcan clay cooking pot) stir-fry the seasoned meat pieces and garlic cloves with salt and pepper in a little olive oil until browned. Add the red pepper and onion, and finally the fennel. Continue to stir-fry gently. Finally, mix in the chips.

Ingredients (for 4 people)

1 small red & 1 small green
  pepper, cut into thin strips
1 potato, peeled and cubed
75 g cooked mussels
75 g cooked peeled prawns
75 g crabmeat sticks, chopped
50 g cooked octopus tentacles,
  chopped
a handful of peas, pre-cooked
2 garlic cloves, crushed
1 bunch fresh fennel, chopped
olive oil; salt & pepper

Ingredients (for 4 people)

lambs liver and lung (ask the
  butcher for *carn de frit*; he
  will know how much you
  need), chopped into squares,
  seasoned with fresh thyme
1 red pepper, finely sliced
1 onion, roughly chopped
1 large potato, cut into chips
small piece of fresh fennel,
  chopped
several garlic cloves, whole
salt & pepper
chilli to garnish (optional)

This relatively easy, although long walk takes you from mountain heights down towards the plain through ever-changing landscapes — rocky mountain trails, woodlands and streams, craggy gorges and sweeping valleys. The mountain refuge of Tossals Verds at the half-way mark is beautifully sited.

tossals verds
WALK

Start the walk at **km34 on the Ma10**: walk down the road from the **Cúber Lake** towards the Gorg Blau. Where the water channel (*'Tubería'* on the map) goes under the road, head northeast on the maintenance path alongside it, signposted to 'Font d'es Prat' and 'Tossals Verds'. Admire the magnificent views down over the **Gorg Blau** as you contour round the mountain slopes.

Eventually you come to a **bridge** signposted 'Tossals Verds' (**50min**). Cross the bridge and continue up through the woods on the old cobbled steps (the ancient

Distance: 16km/10mi; 5h30min-6h

Grade: long, but not difficult; an ascent of 100m/330ft up to the Coll d'es Coloms, then a descent of 650m/2130ft, mostly on good trails and tracks (last 2h on tarmac)

Equipment: hiking boots, water, suncream, sunhat, warm clothing in winter

Transport: 08.00 🚌 or 07.30 🚐 L211 to Sóller, then 🚐 IB-15 from Sóller to Lake Cúber (departs Plaça d'América at 09.10). Return by 🚌 from Lloseta to Palma (Inca-Palma line, every 30min)

Refreshments en route: mountain refuge of Tossals Verds, halfway through the walk

Points of interest:
Font d'es Prat de Massanella (spring and aqueduct)
Bestard Mountain Boots at Lloseta

wayfarers' route from Sóller to Lluc), passing various *sitjas* (round earthen mounds where charcoal was once burned). Soon you reach the **Coll d'es Coloms** (Pigeons' Pass). Just over the col, ignore the signposted path off right into the woods, towards the rough summit of the Tossals mountain. Continue gently downhill through a dappled landscape of holm oak woods.

More **wooden signposts** appear (**1h05min**). Your ongoing

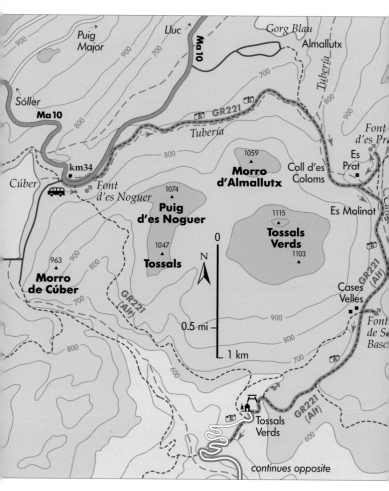

continues opposite

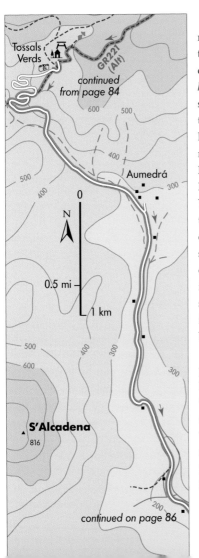

continued
from page 84

Aumedrá

N

0.5 mi

1 km

▲ **S'Alcadena**
816

continued on page 86

route to Tossals continues down a couple of stone steps, but first *keep left*, following the signs to 'Font d'es Prat', to arrive at one of Mallorca's most famous mountain springs, the **Font d'es Prat de Massanella (1h15min)**. You'll find it hiding at the back of a wide clearing — a small stone arch where the crystal clear waters flow below the stone step just inside; you can fill up your water bottles here.

Return to the signposts and drop down left now towards 'Tossals Verds' along a shaded earthen path. This route takes you through a very pretty landscape of woodlands and streams, and

85

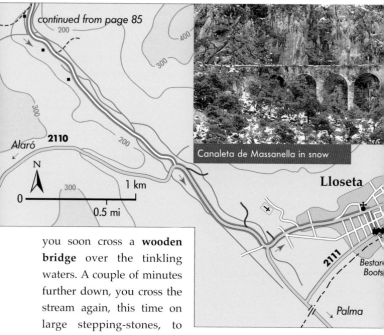

continued from page 85

Alaró **2110**

Lloseta

Bestar
Boots

Palma

Canaleta de Massanella in snow

you soon cross a **wooden bridge** over the tinkling waters. A couple of minutes further down, you cross the stream again, this time on large stepping-stones, to continue along a beautiful old rocky trail as it rounds the eastern face of the large craggy Tossals mountain. Where the trail makes a sharp bend down to the left and then to the right, lift your eyes for a minute to look across to the rocky crags opposite, and you will see the old aqueduct which was built to carry the famous **Canaleta de Massanella** down to the plain — this is the best view of it (see above).

By now panoramic views of the plain have opened up, and

the route eventually becomes less rocky. You pass through a gap in an old stone wall and emerge on the slopes of **Sa Basola** where, just uphill from the path, the old **well** of Sa Basola sits on an open incline (**1h45min**). This is a very pretty place in spring, when the field

Descent from the Tossals Verds refuge

is a mass of high pink asphodels blowing in the breeze.

Refreshed after a drink, continue along the grassy path over the brow of the hill, passing the ruins of an old farmstead (**Les Cases Velles**) down to the right. Far-reaching vistas ahead show you the distant green fields of the Orient Valley and, to the right, high rocky ridges — from Tossals mountain to the L'Ofre peak. Below you lies a once-farmed, secluded valley, where there are still a few almond trees on the terraced slopes, and drystone walls reach high up the hillside. At **1h55min** ignore a rough path up left off the main path; this little-used route disappears over the brow of the hill.

Continuing along the stony path, you find yourself in a 'rock garden' — all manner of flowering shrubs border the way — bright yellow gorse bushes, wild thyme, wild sage, *Euphorbias* and *Hypericum* throw splashes of colour over the limestone rocks, as you descend ever more gently towards the next valley.

Heading towards the Tossals mountain refuge after a winter snowfall

Further down, the path begins a more serious descent, twisting and turning through a series of rocky bends, down to the mountain refuge of **Tossals Verds (2h20min)**. If you've done your homework and ordered your meal in advance, Paquita will have the table set, and a wonderful aroma of home-cooking will quicken your senses as you walk in the door! Why not enjoy coffee afterwards outside in the garden?

To continue on down towards the plain, leave the refuge by the large gates and start down the lane. After about 100m/yds, turn left down a signposted donkey trail, which cuts off some bends. Rejoining the winding lane, continue down through a myriad of olive trees on sloping terraces. The lane snakes between the high sides of a very impressive gorge, crosses a boulder-strewn stream via a **bridge**, and comes down into foothills. At a small parking area at **Aumedrá** (**3h30min**), climb a stile over a fence, then continue along a tarmac lane. Cross a small bridge and continue through fields and woodlands. It is now fairly level walking, with the stream bed on your left; soon you can see the impressive rocky pine-covered cliffs of S'Alcadena to the right — one of the twin bluffs visible from L'Ofre peak or the plain.

Bestard Mountain Boots factory & shop
C/ Estació 40-42, 07360, Lloseta.   www.bestard.com
(971 514044/fax 971 514414
Why not visit this shop to see their huge selection of high-quality mountain boots and footwear ... available at irresistible prices! Walk past the station and go over the bridge (signposted to Bestard Boots). Considered among Europe's 'Top Ten', Bestard have been making boots on Mallorca since 1940, starting out as a small family enterprise. You'll find all types of outdoor footwear here and experts to advise and fit you.

Eventually the narrow lane meets the Ma2110 (the **Lloseta/Alaró road**; **4h45min-5h**) on a wide bend. Keep straight ahead, then take the first road off left, signed to Inca. Turn right after 1km, in the centre of **Lloseta**, on pedestrianised **Mestre Antoni Vidal**. Then cross the main Ma2111, to find the **station** almost opposite, just to the left (**5h30min-6h**). But first you might like to visit Bestard Boots, just a stone's throw away.

Refugi Tossals Verds

This lovely restored stone refuge was inaugurated in April 1995 — the first in a series of mountain huts to be opened along the 'Ruta de Pedra en Sec' (Drystone Route) extending across the Tramuntana mountain range from north to south.

At 540m, and surrounded by high craggy mountains, it also has far-reaching views down over the Orient Valley.

It costs 11 € per person to spent a night in the dormitory on bunk-beds with your own sleeping sack, but for an extra 4 € you can have sheets and towels. There is only one private double room (complete with bathroom!), at 39 € (for two people) per night.

Meals prices are: breakfast 4.50 €, lunch 10.50 €, salad 4.50 €, supper 8 €, picnic 6.50 €

Please book ahead if you want lunch or supper; it's not that easy for the cook to bring provisions up to the refuge, and no cook likes to waste food! You also have the option of bringing your own food. You can barbecue it on the outdoor fireplace; there are tables and benches, and plenty of space, plus a sheltered barbecue area with running water.

> **REFUGI TOSSALS VERDS**
> **Correspondence to: Apartat de Correus 41/07360, Lloseta, Mallorca (971 173700 for information and booking overnight stays. You can also book online in English at www.conselldemallorca.net/mediambient/pedra**
> **open daily all year round** €
> *Meals must be booked in advance!*
>
> The main Sunday lunch is a particularly scrumptious version of **arròs brut**, with salad if you like.
>
> From Mondays to Saturdays there is a different set menu every day, which varies according to provisions.
>
> Any day of the week they will also happily prepare a hefty plate of **pa amb oli**, the Mallorcan 'snack' shown on page 7.
>
> And of course, you can always buy cold drinks, tea or coffee, etc.

restaurants

eat

The cheerful dining room at Tossals Verds

The *arròs brut* at Tossals Verds is certainly excellent. Opposite is my son Julian's recipe for you to try out — it's not difficult to make and, as you can imagine, the possibilities for varying ingredients are almost endless. It's always delicious.

Remember that, like so many other recipes in this book, the dish is best cooked in a *greixonera,* a Mallorcan clay cooking pot which you can use on the hob *and* put in the oven. Why not buy one at Inca market (Excursion 2) and take it home?

Setas are commonly found in Mallorcan supermarkets all year round, but you won't get them back home. Try porcini mushrooms, which are usually available dry.

recipes

eat

'Dirty' rice (arròs brut)

Stir-fry the pieces of meat in olive oil in the *greixonera* until golden brown. Add the onion, peppers and celery and stir-fry, then add the *setas*, the (optional) snails and the herbs — *except for* the tumeric and parsley.

Pour in the wine, and turn down the heat so that this simmers for about 5min. Now add 200 ml of water per person and bring to the boil. Put in the liver at this stage, so that it cooks through. Throw in the rice and the green beans and, while they boil gently, add a sprinkling of tumeric powder. Lift out the liver.

Lastly, ladle a cupful of the broth into a small bowl. Add the parsley and garlic. Mash up the liver and add to the small bowl mixture. When you think the rice is just cooked, turn off the heat and pour in the contents of the small bowl. Let stand a few minutes, then serve piping hot!

Ingredients (for 4 people)
400 g mixed meat, chopped up (rabbit, pork, chicken)
1 chicken liver
1 medium onion, finely chopped
1 red & 1 green pepper, finely chopped
2 stalks green celery, finely chopped
several sprigs of fresh parsley, chopped
100 g fresh green beans
200 g *setas* (wild mushrooms), sliced
salt & pepper
olive oil
2 cloves garlic, crushed
thyme, rosemary, basil, bay leaf (to taste)
dash of powdered turmeric
150 ml white or red wine
200 g rice
1 dozen snails (optional!)

This is the perfect route if weather is threatening on higher levels or if you fancy a fairly easy but interesting circular walk. The route boasts beautiful mountain panoramas, some local culture (both natural and historical), and ends up with a wonderful meal inside Lluc's huge monastery.

around lluc monastery

WALK

Start the walk at the **Lluc car park**, taking the road back out of the monastery. After just over 200m/yds, turn left into a wide entrance. Then turn right immediately, along a path past a **stone house**, and go through the gate of the **football pitch**. Leave the pitch via another narrow metal gate at the far left end.

Joining a wide track, go left, to cross a **wooden bridge** over the stream bed. On the far side you'll find your narrow path. It runs between

Distance: 9km/5.6mi; 3h15min

Grade: easy, with an ascent of 220m/720ft

Equipment: hiking boots or stout walking shoes, sunhat, water, warm clothing in winter

Transport: 🚂 to Inca, connecting 🚌 L332 to Lluc monastery. Return the same way.

Refreshments:
Restaurant 'Sa Fonda' inside Lluc Monastery; café just outside in the square (at start and end of the walk)

Points of interest:
Lluc Monastery
Camel Rock
Ca S'Amitger information centre

boulders and up some ancient cobbled steps (part of the centuries-old mountain route between Lluc and Pollença). You rise up onto level ground by a *sitja* (circular earthen mound where charcoal was once burned; **15min**), where a signpost on the right indicates a short foray to the famous Camel Rock (**Es Camell**). It only takes about five minutes to wind between the rocks to this natural limestone sculpture; personally I think it looks much more like a dinosaur.

Back at the *sitja*, continue gently uphill to a **junction** (**20min**), where you veer slightly left to continue ahead along the wide, open track. Just over the rise, a **viewpoint with stone seats** invites you to take a break and admire the splendid view

95

Es Camell (Camel Rock)
Camel Rock, about 20min from Lluc, is a typical karst rock formation, caused by the action of rainwater, carbon dioxide and other elemental forces such as low temperatures, which dissolve the calcareous rock. The soft rock striates, and some of the edges are knife-sharp! These particular rocks have taken on the shape of a huge animal. Below right: the 'enchanted wood' is an ideal place to look for wild orchids.

towards the huge massif opposite — Puig Roig (Red Mountain; 1003m), with Puig Femenias (920m) to its right.

The track now descends a couple of bends and soon becomes a very pleasant walk through an 'enchanted wood', passing many weird and wonderful rock formations. Later it winds up to a **campsite** called **Es Pixarell (40min)**, with running water and toilet facilities. From here you enjoy an excellent open vista towards Puig Major, Mallorca's highest peak. Walk up the rough tarmac lane for a few minutes to the Ma10, and turn left (caution: oncoming traffic), to find the next **picnic area** on the other side of the

road a few minutes further along.

From the picnic area, go down some stone steps to the right of the WCs and turn left at the bottom, to walk through the trees

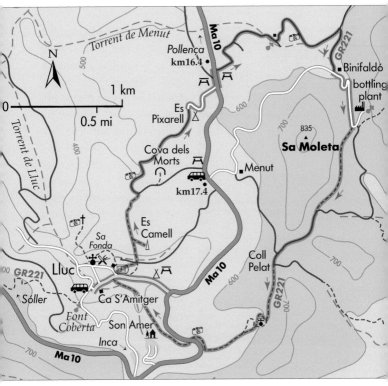

between more picnic tables and barbecue areas. At the far end, veer slightly to the right: a couple of minutes up the slope will put you on the wide forestry track towards Pollença (it's just beyond the rustic **wooden gate** that exits onto the Ma10). Turn right uphill, over the rise, to follow this pleasant woodland walk. The track bends down to the left before heading right

Top: the 'Sant Pere' oak near Binifaldó is reputed to be 500 years old. Below: the 14th-century pilgrims' rooms at Lluc Monastery, with accommodation for travellers above and stables and troughs below

again (ignore a wide but faint track off to the right near some poplars). You will come to a small **spring and water channel** on a bend (**1h10min**); turn left here, passing a restored **stone hut**. The trail now becomes rockier and climbs up through the trees for another 10 minutes or so, before opening out in more scrubland — with a splendid view towards the huge Tomir mountain rising up directly ahead of you. The route then rises much more gently, to a wide level track (**1h30min**), another part of the original Lluc/Pollença route and now part of the **GR221**.

Turn right, and after a few minutes come to the big house of **Binifaldó**, a natural environment education centre. A **GR signpost** pointing right indicates a shorter — mostly tarmac — route back to Lluc, so go left, and rise up to the

Ca S'Amitger (Serra de Tramuntana Information Centre)
Plaça dels Pelegrins s/n, 07315, Lluc
(/fax 971 517070; e-mail: amitger@
dgmambie.caib.es. Daily ex 25/12 and
1/1, from 09.00-16.30. Entry free
This information centre is housed in a
building that dates from the 16th
century; the interior was restored in
1992. It was once the house of (ca'n)
an amitger — a person who acted as
mediator between a landowner and
his beneficiaries. Inside is a wealth of
information about natural science,
flora and fauna, with audio-visual aids.
A special section is dedicated to the
black vulture (voltor negre) and other
birds of prey. It is a fascinating place.
Right: coming up to the old Lluc/
Pollença route near Binifaldó

gates of the **Binifaldó water-bottling plant (1h50min)**, on your left.

Go straight ahead; a stile takes you over a low wall by another gate. Take the GR path to the right (for 'Lluc'); this twists away over the hills, dipping and rising through the woods. When you meet a wide track (**2h10min**), turn right, rise steeply over a hill, and walk back into the woods.

Go left at a signposted junction, cross some *sitjas,* and then veer right over a low stone wall. Follow the GR waymarks downhill, back towards the Lluc valley, with excellent views of the double-peaked Massanella mountain. On meeting the main Ma10 road (**2h55min**), follow GR signs to pass the **Son Amer** refuge and continue back to **Lluc** (**3h15min**) … and **Sa Fonda!**

Sa Fonda

Lluc is a very popular place with visitors and hikers alike, and Sa Fonda offers just the right lively, warm and welcoming atmosphere — especially in winter when there's a fire. It's cosy in spite of its size, and the elegant marble columns and arches, and the wooden beams give it real character. How pleasant to stay here overnight, enjoying a splendid dinner with plenty of wine, and knowing that you only have to climb a few steps to get 'home'.

SA FONDA
Santuari de Lluc (/fax 971 517022
from 09.00-23.00 daily ex Sun evenings and Mon €€

specialities include mountain-reared roast **kid**, roast **suckling pig** and **paella**

plenty of starters to choose from: **salads**, **prawns** in garlic, **squid**, **chicken croquettes**, *frits*, **snails** and more

soups, **egg** dishes and **fish**

apart from the specialities, other **meat** choices could be grilled **lamb** chops, sirloin **steak**, **pork** fillets wrapped in cabbage leaves

and plenty of **desserts** …

restaurants

eat

Santuari de Lluc (Lluc monastery)

07315 Lluc ℂ 971 871525/fax 971 517096; e-mail: info@lluc.net

The monastery, steeped in legend and history, was founded in the 8th century according to legend — the 13th century according to history books — when a small chapel was built. The present buildings date from the 17th and 18th centuries. The church, built between 1622 and 1684, was considerably altered at the beginning of the 1900s.

Lluc is an important Roman Catholic sanctuary; visitors come here from all over the island, and pilgrimages are often made on foot up to Lluc. The museum contains coin collections, typical costumes, and items of archaeological interest found in the cave of Cometa dels Morts northeast of Es Camell.

Staying overnight at the monastery is both comfortable and exciting, if you don't mind being awakened by the clanging bells in the courtyard at early hours!

Prawns in garlic *(gambas al ajillo)*; not illustrated

This starter is simplicity itself. For four people you will need 1 kg peeled prawns, 4 crushed garlic cloves and some chopped chives. Heat some olive oil in a small frying pan, add the prawns and stir-fry for a couple of minutes. Then add the garlic and the finely chopped chives, and stir-fry for a further 2min. Serve piping hot in individual clay dishes.

Cabbage parcels with pork fillet *(llom amb col)*

Some years ago you could find *tords amb col* (thrushes baked in cabbage leaves) on the menu, but since thrush-netting was brought under strict control after entry into the EU, it is hard to find, and doesn't appeal to most people anyway. Today pork is used for this popular dish.

Boil the cabbage leaves until slightly cooked; drain. Gently fry the pork fillets in a little olive oil with some salt and pepper; lift out, and wrap carefully in the semi-cooked cabbage leaves, making little 'parcels' (secure with thick cotton, skewers or tooth-picks). Place in a roasting tin.

Sauté the onions in the same oil, until they become 'watery', and pour over the cabbage parcels. Now bake gently in the oven until the cabbage is soft. (As an option, you could add tomato sauce and prunes, as at Lluc.)

<u>Ingredients (for 4 people)</u>
1 pork fillet per person
plenty of large cabbage leaves
3-4 large onions, finely chopped
olive oil
salt & pepper
handful of prunes (optional)

recipes

eat

Seafood *paella*

'Paella' is named for the cooking vessel, the *paellera*. For this recipe, use a *paellera* for 4 people. Cover the base with olive oil, put over the heat, and stir-fry the onion, chopped red pepper and parsley for 2min. Still stir-frying, add the squid, small prawns, mussels and cockles, then the cubes of fish and garlic; stir-fry for another 2-3min.

Add the giant prawns, crayfish and artichokes; pour over the stock and simmer for 10min. Then remove and set aside the large prawns and crayfish.

Add the rice, green beans and tumeric and bring to the boil. As the rice begins to swell, gradually turn down the heat, to simmer gently (move the rice around with a wooden spatula, so it doesn't stick). The rice should soak up all the liquid; you may have to add a little water to finish cooking the rice, but it should be almost dry when you turn off the heat.

When the rice is 'al dente', turn off the heat, decorate with the prawns, crayfish and strips of red pepper (as above). Cover with a cloth and let stand a good 5min before serving.

Ingredients (for 4 people)
1 onion, finely chopped
2 cloves garlic, crushed
1 tbsp chopped parsley
1 small red pepper, finely chopped
1 large red pepper, roasted,
   skinned and cut into strips
1 artichoke, cut into 8 pieces
handful of fresh green beans
1 squid, chopped in rings
4 giant prawns
4 large crayfish *(cigalas)*
handful small prawns for flavour
12 mussels in their shells
several cockles
200 g cod or monkfish, cubed
olive oil
2 cups rice
1 l fish or vegetable stock
salt & pepper
1 tsp tumeric powder (or saffron)

This delightful country walk is beautiful at any time of year. Puig d'en Marron is draped in a thick blanket of evergreen pine forests, and the hills are riddled with caves containing silent memories of a Moorish past. Two pleasant places to eat at Santa Eugènia should round off your day nicely.

santa eugènia
WALK

Start the walk from the **bus stop** in **Santa Eugènia**: walk back towards 'Santa Maria' along the Ma3040; you will pass **Ca Na Cantona** — your lunch stop at the end of the walk — and leave the village. Just as you leave the last houses, come to **Vinya Taujana** (literally translated as 'Santa Eugenian wine') on the right-hand side of the road, where you can drop in for a coffee, or some interesting wine-tasting along with a bit of *pa amb oli* — a good start to the walk!

Distance: 7.5km/ 4.7mi; 3h

Grade: easy, with gentle ascents of under 180m/ 600ft

Equipment: stout walking shoes, sunhat, water, insect repellent, warm clothing in winter

Transport: 🚌 (Palma/ Inca line) to Santa Maria; connects with 🚌 L311 to Santa Eugènia. Return the same way.

Refreshments:
Vinya Taujana wine *celler* and Bar/ restaurante Ca Na Cantona, both in Santa Eugènia

Point of interest:
caves at Ses Coves

Continue along the road as far as the turn off to 'Ses Coves' (**20min**), and follow this narrow country lane up towards the hills, veering round left at the top to come into the picturesque hamlet of **Ses Coves** (**30min**), privileged with far-reaching views across the plain. Keep straight ahead now, following the lane as it dips down behind the houses, passing a **cave** on the left with an ancient **wine-press** inside; a wooden door just to the right of the old press, jammed shut and overgrown, hides the entrance to a large cool cave where vats were once stored, now home to some white owls.

The lane twists to the right, widens by an old **well**, and narrows again. On coming to a T-junction (**40min**), go left

through a little valley, dotted with cottages amidst orange groves and flowering fields. You will reach the gated entrance to **Puig d'en Marron** on the right (**45min**). This is usually locked, but there is an access gap to the left of the gate, and so your gentle climb to the top now begins. In spring the beautiful song of the nightingale can be heard echoing in the pine-scented silence; you may spot a variety of other birds and see little rabbits scurrying away into the bushes as your footsteps disturb their peace. Looking to the right after the first

Cave with wine press at Ses Coves and lane on Puig d'en Marron; below: fields near Santa Eugènia

bend in the track, you can see other caves on the soft sandstone hillside across the valley.

Eventually the route divides (**1h05min**) into two earthen tracks. The route ahead goes through the woods between some weekend dwellings and descends the hill on the south side without much of interest, so take the right-hand turn to continue on the main track. Keep right at each fork for about another 15 minutes. Now on level ground, continue along the main track until it veers left in front of a **tall wire fence**, passes a small house with a huge **gate** and then veers right, emerging in **open fields** as a grassy path.

Keep along the path, passing an elevated **triangulation**

point (320m; **1h25min**) somewhat obscured by a clump of trees on the left. Further along the path, walk past a very tall metallic **firewatch tower**, and come down to a wide clearing with a stone wall on the right, from where there are some good views down over Palma Bay and the airport runways.

To return, retrace your steps back down the mountain, as far as the gated entrance to the *puig*. Back in the valley (**2h10min**), turn sharp right (the opposite direction from which you came), to continue along the lane. Set back above on the hillside, a huge mound of large boulders marks the site of an ancient **Moorish**

burial ground. Continue uphill now and, after about 150m/yds, turn left downhill at a fork, passing the gated, arched entrance to an old well. Just after this, pass the access drive to a house and then turn left alongside the outer wall of the property down a path through the orchard. A red paint spot marks the beginning of your narrow path up the hillside. In only about five minutes you rise up to a **rocky pass** (before climbing up through the pass, be sure to take a look back at the view to the south).

I call this the 'Shangri-La Pass', because the path comes up from this lovely little valley, but once through, all stillness is left behind, as winds whipping across the plain catch at your clothing. Now climb the low stone wall to the left, to make your way up to the cross monument atop **Puig de Santa Eugènia** (245m; **2h30min**). What a magnificent view! The extensive Tramuntana sierra stretches across a wide horizon, with the plain below and many towns and villages dotted about like a multicoloured patchwork quilt.

To end the walk, go back down over the stone wall, and head down left past a gnarled old pine, through scrub, to a walled-in stony track which you follow to the bottom. Then turn right along the level and after some 200m turn left down the steep rough tarmac. Coming into **Santa Eugènia's main square** (**3h**), continue straight ahead downhill along **Carrer Major**. At the bottom (back at your starting point), turn left along the main road to visit **Ca Na Cantona**.

The cross atop Puig de Santa Eugènia, and the descent back to the village. Opposite: 'Shangri-La Pass'

Vinya Taujana

This delightful wine cellar, run by third-generation vine-growers, produces a variety of Binissalem D.O. (Denominació d'Origen; see page 9) from their native (Manto Negro, Calet, Moll) and foreign (Cabernet Sauvignon, Merlot, Syrah) vines. Visits to the winery can be pre-arranged, but you can call in for a bit of *pa amb oli* or some cheese while you sample some of their excellent wines — it makes a great start to this walk!

Xisca behind the bar, Vinya Taujana

VINYA TAUJANA
C/ Balanguera 40, 07142 Santa Eugènia (/fax 971 144494
closed Mon; Tue-Fri 09.00-13.00 and 16.00-20.00; Sat/Sun 09.00-13.00 €

stop here for a coffee, or sample some wines and have a snack of *pa amb oli*

restaurants

eat

Ca Na Cantona

Pedro and Maria run this little cafeteria, with its typically warm and friendly village atmosphere. It's popular with both the locals and passers-by, since there's always good home cooking available. They have an extra dining room upstairs seating 50 people, where they occasionally cater for large groups — cyclists, walkers, tourists — usually on Sundays. You're sure of a warm welcome here.

CA NA CANTONA
C/ Balanguera 33, 07142 Santa
Eugènia (971 144031
daily ex Thu, 07.00–23.00 €

Maria features Mallorcan cuisine, with **specialities** including **roast suckling pig, roast lamb** and **roast kid, stuffed squids**

plenty of other **meat** or **fish** dishes to choose from: **pork cabbage parcels, seafood-filled marrows, stuffed artichokes** ...

plus simple dishes like **eggs and bacon, omelettes, salads**

You can also get **tapas** here, or snacks — typical Mallorcan pastries such as **cocarrois** (vegetable pasties; recipe overleaf) or **empanadas** (meat pies)

RECIPES FROM CA NA CANTONA

This is how Maria makes her particular version of *tumbet* with pork and her delicious vegetable pasties. I've also included a photo of her stuffed squids, in case you're tempted to try them!

Mallorcan 'ratatouille' with fillet of pork (tumbet de llom)

Fry the pork fillets in a little olive oil, with salt, pepper and the garlic. Lift out the pork and set aside. Next fry the aubergines and the red

pepper with the garlic. Lift out.

Now fry the potatoes until soft, then put in a baking tray or dish. Place the pork fillets over the potatoes, and top with the red pepper and aubergines.

Cover the lot with the chopped tomatoes (if you have time to make your own sauce, skin and chop the tomatoes, then stir-fry

<u>Ingredients (for 4 people)</u>
4 pork fillets
1 large red pepper, in large pieces
2 aubergines, sliced 1 cm thick
2 or 3 potatoes, thinly sliced
2 garlic cloves, whole
400 g chopped tomato sauce
1 bay leaf
olive oil
salt & pepper

Below: Maria's stuffed squids

them slowly with salt, pepper, a bay leaf and a little olive oil; otherwise use a 400 g tin). Put in the bay leaf, and bake in a moderate oven (180°C/350°F/gas mark 4) for about 10-15min.

Vegetable pasties *(cocarrois)*

To make the pastry, put the butter or lard and water in a bowl, then fold in sufficient flour (with a pinch of salt) to knead into a soft dough. Make small balls of dough, and roll out into an oval shape, ready to fill.

To prepare the filling, chop up the raw vegetables, add the sultanas, and mix in a little olive oil (about 2 tbsp).

Place the vegetables in the centre of each pastry, and fold over to cover, forming a 'pasty' shape. Place the pasties on a greased baking tray and bake in a slow oven at 150°C/300°F/gas mark 2 until browned.

Ingredients (for 16 pasties)
(for the pastry):
200 g butter or lard, in pieces
250 ml water
plain flour as needed
(for the filling):
2 bunches fresh Swiss chard
1 bunch fresh spinach leaves
5-6 cabbage leaves
6 spring onions
1 small cauliflower, in florets
50 g sultanas
olive oil
salt & pepper

recipes
eat

This adventurous walk from Calvià goes north up the Vall Negre (Black Valley) and climbs the wooded foothills of Son Font, then continues across a high plateau towards Puig de Na Bauçana, a rounded rocky peak from where you can take in all of the Calvià region in an eagle's eye sweep.

calvià to galilea

9 WALK

Start the walk from the bus stop in **Calvià**, from where you go east along **Carrer Major**, following signposting to 'Puigpunyent'. Soon turn left along **Carrer Jaume III** and follow this to a T-junction at the top. Go right to follow the road out of the village, veering left up into the woods.

After passing a large house surrounded by a wall (on a bend to the left), you'll see some **signposts** indicating the walkers' route to 'Galilea' and 'Puigpunyent' (**15min**). Leave the tarmac here, to take the wide sandy track down to the left, beside the wall. The track curves round to the right, and you begin your ascent up the **Vall Negre**. At the top of the

Distance: 12km/7.4mi; 3h30min

Grade: straightforward but strenuous, with an overall ascent of 500m/1640ft; all on good paths and tracks

Equipment: hiking boots, water, sunhat, warm clothing in winter

Transport: 🚌 L111 from Palma to Calvià village (ask for 'Centre vila'). Return on 🚌 L140 from Galilea to Palma (see page 137)

Refreshments en route:
several bar/cafés in Calvià for morning coffee
Bar Parroquial in Galilea (at the end)

Points of interest:
aljubs (Arab water deposits)
Galilea, Mallorca's highest village
Scott's Hotel, Galilea: if you do this walk late in the day, contemplate spending a night at Scott's Hotel above the village — for pampered luxury (see www.scottsgalilea.com), splendid views, and breakfast on the terrace. You can walk back to Calvià the next day.

rise, the route continues along a narrower, earthen track on the right (marked by a **wooden post**) and soon takes you through a wooden gate. Shortly afterwards, you come up to a small clearing where there is an *aljub* — a water catchment. The word *aljub* comes from the Arabic; the Moors built many of these cleverly engineered water deposits during their occupation of

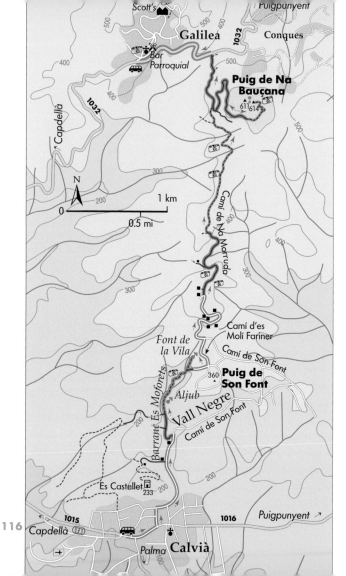

Scott's

Galilea

Puigpunyent

Conques

Bar
Parroquial

Capdellà

1032

**Puig de Na
Bauçana**

611 614

N

0   200   1 km

0.5 mi

300

Camí de Na Morruda

Camí d'es
Molí Fariner

*Font de
la Vila*

Camí de Son Font

**Puig de
Son Font**

360

Aljub

Vall Negre

Camí de Son Font

Barranc Es Moforets

Es Castellet

233

1015

Calvià

Capdellà

Palma

1016

Puigpunyent

the island. Some are still in excellent condition even after a thousand years. Have you ever tried to build a drystone arched roof that would last that long? Calvià's water supply used to come from this *aljub*.

The route continues steeply uphill, clearly waymarked, and higher up you begin to get some good views of the coast. It's not long before the rough trail comes up to join a wider track, where you see some more **signposts** to the 'Aljub d'es Pou Nou' and 'Son Font — Galilea' (**45min**). Here it's worth taking a short detour left, to the **Aljub d'es Pou Nou**, also called the **Font de la Vila** (village spring). It's a pleasant place for a drink stop, also allowing another close inspection of these amazing Moorish constructions. The main route

At about 1h30min the trail, supported by a wall, contours round the head of a ravine.

continues to the right from the signposts, soon coming up to a wooden **gate**, after which the way becomes tarmac.

Walk to the top of the rise and turn left, keeping straight along **Camí d'es Molí Fariner**. This rises to join **Camí de Son Font** (**1h**), where you will find more **signposts**. Go left, to continue ascending between beautiful houses and villas, all with impressive views down over the coastline. You pass between **two stone pillars** where the Camí de Son Font becomes the **Camí de Na Morruda (1h15min)**.

As you continue, now on the level, the rounded sugar-loaf peak of Na Bauçana becomes very obvious directly ahead, and the jagged peak of Galatzó (1026m) thrusts up on the horizon behind the houses of Galilea perched high on the distant ridge. After more **signposts by a wide metal gate**, the route descends through a changed landscape of open fields, with panoramic views across the hills. The stony track is fenced off and well waymarked; it dips and rises, eventually heading into the trees as a narrower path. The woodland path soon changes again, becoming bushland, then later rises onto a wall-supported trail. You contour round the head of a ravine, drawing ever nearer to Na Bauçana and Galilea.

Keep right along the higher, narrow path signposted to 'Galilea', ignoring the gated path to the left (**1h50min**). You join a wide track some five minutes later. Down left leads to Galilea, but first you'll want to conquer the summit! So turn right and then go left up a steep sandy track (where the track straight ahead is private property). After passing a well-preserved **limekiln**, you wind up for some 20 minutes, until you come to a wide gateway leading onto an open grassy plateau just below the peak. And now for the final assault: follow the track across the field, veering left towards the mountain. The track eventually becomes a narrow cairn-marked mountain path, zigzagging up the curious stone steps cut into the rock, snaking its way all the way up to the summit of **Na Bauçana (614m;**

2h30min). Up here, perched by the summit post, you'll need time to take in all that can be seen from this amazing vantage point: Calvià's coastline, the Na Burguesa mountain range to the southwest, villages dotted here and there, Puigpunyent to the north, nestling in the sheltered valley, the jagged peak of Galatzó, Palma Bay, the central plain and the Tramuntana mountain range

Galilea
The highest village on Mallorca, the houses of Galilea sit on a rocky ridge at over 500m, south of the jagged peak of Galatzó (1026m), commanding wonderful views down over the southwest coast. The little church of the Immaculate Conception was built in 1810, and the small but attractive square with the Bar Parroquial is the village meeting place.

stretching away on the northern horizon.

Descend now, back to the wide track, and follow it all the way down, going right at the bottom of the hill, and keeping on down to the road (Ma1032), where you climb over the stile (**3h10min**). Go left to walk up the road into **Galilea** (**3h30min**) and, at the junction, turn up right into the village. The **bus stop** for your return bus is just here at the crossroads, and a minute up left brings you to the tiny square with the little church of the **Immaculate Conception**. Just by the church is the **Bar Parroquia**l, the village meeting place, and from the wall at the end of the square (at almost 500m) there is a fantastic view!

Bar Parroquial

The picturesque little square by the side of Galilea's church houses the Bar Parroquial, where you can get good *tapas*. The small front terrace, adorned with flowering shrubs, is lovely in warm weather, but there is also a larger terrace just up the steps to the right with lovely views over the village. And of course, there is plenty of room inside!

BAR PARROQUIAL
Plaza Pio XII, 1, 07195 Galilea,
(971 614187
closed Mon, otherwise open from
07.00-19.00 €

tapas include squids or octopus in sauce, mushrooms with garlic, meatballs in sauce, Russian salad, etc; also **pa amb oli**, cheese, ham, or **sobrasada** rolls and sandwiches — while the bread lasts!

SCOTTS HOTEL GALILEA
Sa Costa den Mandons 3, 07195
Galilea (971 870100 (UK (0871
717 4227); fax 971 870267
www.scottsgalilea.com

For more information, bookings, and photographs, log on to their website

restaurants

eat

Mallorcan 'pizza' (coca amb verdura)

Grease a pizza tin and cover with a thin layer of dough. Sprinkle over all the chopped ingredients and bake at 190°C/375°F/gas mark 5 until the parsley crisps at the edges (about 15-20min).

Deep-fried baby squids (xipirons)

Sprinkle the inside of the squids with salt & pepper, roll in flour and deep fry a few minutes until golden brown. Serve sprinkled with lemon juice.

Scrambled eggs with prawns (revolt de gambes)

Fry the prawns and spring onion (and optional garlic) in a little olive oil for a minute, then add the eggs. Stir-fry with a spatula until scrambled, adding the chives just at the finish.

Ingredients *for the 'pizza'*
thin pastry base (buy it, or use the same ingredients as for the pasties on page 113)
1 onion, thinly sliced
1 spring onion, chopped
1 red pepper, in fine strips
small bunch parsley, chopped

for the squids (for 4 people)
12-16 small squids, cleaned
flour
salt & pepper
lemon juice

for the eggs (for 4 people)
6 eggs, seasoned with salt & pepper, and beaten
200 g peeled cooked prawns
1 spring onion, chopped
chopped chives to taste
1 clove crushed garlic (optional)

recipes

eat

Palma is a beautiful Mediterranean city, full of architectural and cultural walks (see leaflets at tourist offices). But I designed this circuit to give more insight into Palma's varied and cosmopolitan character, bringing in elements of past, present and future — and a spectacular 'aerial' view from magnificently sited Bellver Castle.

palma city
WALK

The walk starts at the **stop for tourist bus 50**, below the imposing **Almudaina Palace** [2], a royal residence for Mallorcan kings since the 13th century. Walk north along Avinguda Antoni Maura to **Plaça de la Reina** (with a huge fountain), where all the other buses stop (you can also start here). Standing on the west side of the *plaça,* with your back to the seafront, walk through an archway and into the old town, following **Carrer de la Mar**. Turn right along **Carrer Vallseca**, pass the vegetarian restaurant Flor de Loto, Persian and Italian restaurants, then turn right again on **Carrer Sant Joan**. At the next corner, go left — but not before admiring the splendid façade of **Abaco** [25]. This is a

See plan inside front cover to start and end the walk.

Distance: 6.5km/4mi; 3h15min

Grade: easy; mostly on asphalt. Gentle ascent of some 100m/300ft on an earthen path up to Bellver Castle, descent via steps

Equipment: good walking shoes

Transport: tourist 🚌 50, or 🚌 6, 15 or 17 to Plaça de la Reina (near the cathedral)

Refreshments en route:
plenty of bars, including
bar/restaurants at Es Baluard Museum and the Santa Catalina Market
restaurants at the Pueblo Español
picnic areas in Bellver Park
bars and restaurants on the Passeig Marítim
La Bóveda restaurants/tapas bars at the end of the walk (there are two)

Points of interest:
Es Baluard Museum and city walls
Santa Catalina Market
Pueblo Español
Bellver Castle and park

late-night drinks bar inside an elegant Mallorcan townhouse full of exquisite antique furniture, where fresh exotic fruits and flowers cascade down the main staircase and fill every corner. Visitors are free to wander wherever they wish (expensive fruit

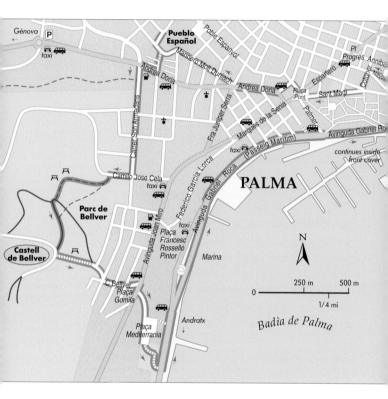

drink in hand), to the accompaniment of soft classical music.

Continue left along **Carrer Apuntadors**, and keep ahead past the square and the hotel Palau Sa Font, then turn left down **Carrer del Ví**. These dark and narrow Spanish alleyways, part of the old walled city, are slowly being restored — but some,

Es Baluard Museum
Plaza Porta de Santa Catalina
s/n, 07012 Palma de Mallorca
(971 908200/fax 971 908203;
museo@esbaluard.org.
Closed Mon, 25th/26th Dec
and New Year's day; otherwise open 16/6-30/9 from
10.00-24.00; 1/10-15/6 from
10.00-24.00
This museum of contemporary
and modern art, inaugurated
on 30th January 2004, contains some 350 works of art,
mostly paintings, sketches and
pieces of sculpture. Among
others, you can see paintings
by Joan Miró, drawings by
Cezanne, Toulouse-Lautrec
and Gaugin, or ceramics by
Picasso. There is also a shop-
library, a bar and a restaurant. The entrance fee is 6 €
(concessions available).

like Carrer del Ví, could still be used in an historical film! At the end, go right on **Carrer de Sant Pere** and, at the end, walk up the steps. You come to part of the **old city wall and one of the bastions** (**25min**), over-looking the harbour and the busy Passeig Marítim below, with Bellver Castle atop the hill to the west. This corner of the ancient city wall has been taken over by the new modern-istic museum of **Es Baluard** (the Bastion; [5] on the plan), where visitors can walk around the para-pets, but just here you can climb the metal staircase up to a higher level for a good view over the city.

Return to the street and go left, rising to **Plaça de La Porta de Santa Catalina** (**30min**), a wide square with an 'upside-down' house in the centre! Bear left, passing the entrance to Es Baluard, then go left again, over a bridge across the Riera stream bed — from where there is an excellent view of the high city walls. Keep ahead, past a park on the left, to reach a main road, **Avinguda Argentina**. Turn left downhill here, and cross at the first pedestrian crossing. Continue along **Carrer d'Annibal**, to arrive at the **Mercat de Santa Catalina** [6] on the next corner (**40min**). Go through the automatic doors and explore. Maybe you fancy

Pueblo Español
C/ Capitán Mesquida Veny 39, Palma de
Mallorca. ℂ 971 237075; Bus routes 4, 5.
Open 09.00-18.00 (17.00 in winter).
www.mallorcawebsite.com

The Pueblo Español (Spanish Town) lets
you visit all the important monuments of
Spain in one day! Built in the late 1960s,
it contains replicas of some of Spain's
most famous places — like the Alhambra
in Granada (above), El Greco's house in
Toledo, the Golden Tower of Seville, the
Arabic Baths of Granada, etc. Full of
narrow Spanish alleys, *plazas*, monuments, restaurants, handicraft shops,
patios and gardens … you'll find this a
very interesting visit.

a Mallorcan pastry? Or a
coffee at the stand-up bar?

Leave the market by the
west doors (diagonally opposite from where you came
in). Coming out on **Carrer Navegació**, go right. Cross over the
first junction, to go left along **Carrer Cotoner**, and then take the
second right turn on **Carrer Sant Magí**. Follow this all the way

to the end, arriving at the wide square of **Plaça del Pont** (**1h**). Cross to the other side, and go left, to come to a wide avenue, **Andrea Doria.** Turn up right here and go up the right-hand side as far as the traffic lights on a bend. Leave the wide avenue here, and continue straight ahead along **Calle del Marinero Moll Duniach**, signposted to the 'Pueblo Español' — you can already see a Spanish tower ahead of you. At the top, veer left around the walled enclosure, and keep left to find the gated entrance to the **Pueblo Español** opposite the Palacio de Congresos (**1h25min**). Allow time for your visit — there's lots to see!

Return to the road, going left, then cross over a bridge and go up some stone steps, back onto Andrea Doria (don't take the right-hand flight of steps leading to some apartments). Turn right, uphill, to the next traffic lights (**1h40min**) and cross over, passing a petrol station and continuing along **Carrer Son Armadans**. This is a pleasant stretch past up-market residences and the 3-star Araxa Hotel. When you come to the crossroads with **Carrer Camilo Jose Cela** (**1h50min**), turn right. Follow this uphill for 100m/yds, to the wide gated entrance to Bellver Park and Castle.

Immediately through the gate, go left up some steps — this is your wooded walk up to the castle (taking the road is a long way round and very tiring). Follow the earthen path uphill through picturesque woodlands — a pleasant change from the asphalt. The path becomes rockier and widens out higher up. Near the top, you pass a large picnic area with benches and tables and a children's play-park; the way veers left and passes another picnic area. Keep ahead across a track, and pass a

Bellver Castle

Bosc de Bellver s/n, 07015 Palma de Mallorca;
(971 730657/Fax 971 454373; www.
mallorcawebsite.com. In summer open Mon-Sat
from 08.00-21:00; Sun/holidays in Apr/May/
Jun/Sep from 10.00-19.00; Sun/holidays in
Jul/Aug from 10.00-14.00 and 16.00-20.00. In
winter (Oct-Mar) open Mon-Sat from 08.00-
20.00; Sun/holidays from 10.00-17.00. Entry fee
2 €, concessions 0,90 €

Bellver Castle has watched over the city of
Palma for some 700 years from its privileged
situation on a wooded hill at 114m above the
bay. Its construction was begun by King Jaime II
in the early 1300s, originally as a royal
residence, although in later centuries it became
a prison. It is the only round castle in all of
Spain, and has three large towers that surround
a central two-storey courtyard — the ground
floor with Romanesque and the upper floor with
Gothic arches. It now contains an important
historical museum covering four periods, from
talaiotic (prehistoric) through to Roman, Islamic
and Medieval times.

monument to the Rotary Club. Cross the track again, and finally follow the stone steps up to the **Castell de Bellver (2h20min)**.

A magnificent panorama lies below. The great white city of Palma spreads out lazily in the sun, embracing the deep blue harbour full of white yachts and colourful mercantile ships, with the hills and mountains beyond. Visit the castle and climb the towers for an even more inspiring view.

Directly below the castle entrance, go back down the steps to the right and descend the long stairway winding through the Bellver woods (with picnic areas). You will probably notice the loud squawking of the colourful parakeets flitting from tree to tree. Go through the gates at the bottom, and continue downhill along **Carrer de Bellver**.

On coming to a main road, turn right. At the traffic lights at **Plaça Gomila**, cross over and keep ahead, but then bear left along the red-paved road. Go past another wide square with lots of parked cars, towards a rounded brick archway, the entrance to a public park. Go through and down the steps to the left, between water fountains and lily ponds, pretty flower beds, and strangely-shaped trees.

Passeig Sagrera

Before you know it, you're down on the seafront (**2h 45min**), on Palma's world-famous **Passeig Marítim**. Cross over for a splendid walk round the bay — past luxury hotels and yacht clubs, expensive shops, ballrooms and nightclubs, Palma's auditorium and countless cafés (of which the 'in' place as I write is the 'Capuccino'). Later you pass below Es Baluard and the

Sa Llotja — a Gothic masterpiece

city wall where you stood earlier, and come to the beautiful façade of **Sa Llotja** [4] (Spanish: La Lonja) — a masterpiece of 15th-century Gothic architecture surrounded by tall elegant palms.

Cross back now, to find **Sa Bóveda** for a genuine Spanish *tapas* lunch. In fact there are two! One of them, just off the Passeig, is open all year round: walk up into **Plaça Llotja** and veer right on **Carrer Botería** — it's just around the corner [23]. The other, mostly open only in fine weather, is on the Passeig itself — just past Plaça Llotja, set back off a small patio [24]. A couple of minutes from either restaurant will bring you back to your starting point opposite the **Almudaina Palace (3h15min)**.

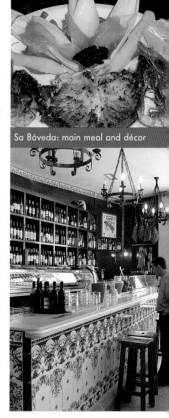

Sa Bóveda: main meal and décor

Sa Bóveda tapas bars and restaurants

In both you'll find delicious, mouth-watering *tapas* and snacks, as well as a few main dishes, like the beautifully presented fish platter shown here. The best idea is to order a variety of *tapas* and a bit of *pa amb oli,* plus a beer or some wine, and you'll feel wonderfully replenished … everything at Bóveda is so tasty.

SA BOVEDA (two locations)
C/ Botería 3, Palma (971 714863, fax 971 712163
daily ex Sun/holidays and Feb from 13.30-16.30 and 20.30-11.45 (00.30 Fri/Sat); open Easter Thu/Fri €€

Passeig Sagrera 3, Palma (971 720026, fax 971 712163
daily, ex Sun/holidays in summer only 13.30-16.30 and 20.30-11.45 (00.30 Fri/Sat); also open in winter if weather is good! €€

tapas include squids fried in batter, stuffed mussels, scrambled egg with mushrooms, fried green peppers, cured ham, goats' cheese in olive oil, small deep-fried fishes, olives and pickles, spanish omelette, fried prawns, steamed mussels, tripe in sauce, mushrooms in garlic

other **snacks** — sandwiches, **pa amb oli**; a few **main dishes** and **desserts**

---

restaurants

eat

A morning out by train, visiting one the island's biggest street markets, in Inca, where you can buy almost anything — from hand-made leather goods to embroidery, tools, toys, fresh vegetables and fruit, pots, pans, sculptures, art, antiques ... than finish with lunch at one of Inca's recommended *celler* restaurants.

inca market

2

EXCURSION

Transport: 🚂 from Palma station to/from Inca (half-hourly); journey time 30min

Refreshments:
Palma railway station café
Celler Ca'n Ripoll or Celler Sa Travesa in Inca

NB: Inca market, Thu only

In only half an hour you travel straight across the plain through open countryside and past various villages, to Inca — Mallorca's third largest town. Coming out of Inca station, you can already see the markets stalls straight ahead down the road opposite, **Avinguda del Bisbe Llompart**, from where you can begin your market tour through the narrow streets, squares, and wider avenues. There's so much to see! From time to time the evocative strains of pan-pipe music fill the air: South American Indians, colourful in their national dress, play their lovely homeland music from the Andes. There are plenty of outdoor cafés where you can stop for refreshments. But before your train journey back to the city, why not drop into one of the typical Mallorcan restaurants I recommend for a superb lunch ?

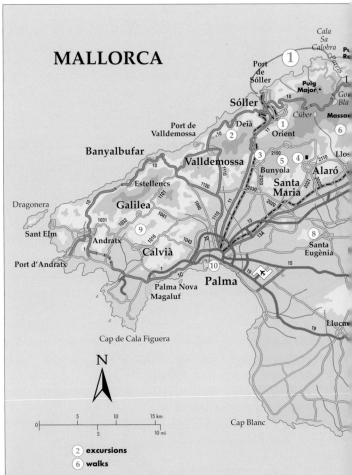

MALLORCA

Cala
Sa
Calobra

Pt
Ro

Port
de
Sóller

Puig
Major

Go
Bla

Sóller

10

Cúber

Massa

Port de
Valldemossa

Deià

2

11

1

Orient

6

Banyalbufar

Valldemossa

3

2100

4

5

2110

Llos

Estellencs

Bunyola

**Santa
Maria**

2020

Alaró

2030

1120

2020

Galilea

1031

1032

1041

11

2021

Dragonera

1101

1040

1110

13

8

1016

1043

9

20

134

Santa
Eugènia

Sant Elm

Andratx

Calvià

19

Port d'Andratx

1

10

Palma

15

Palma Nova
Magaluf

19

Cap de Cala Figuera

Llucm

19

N

0   5   10   15 km

5   10 mi

Cap Blanc

② excursions

⑥ walks

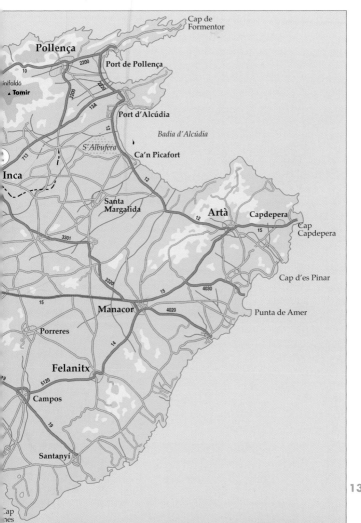

Cap de Formentor

Pollença

2200

Port de Pollença

3220

inifaldó

▲ Tomir

2200

13A

Port d'Alcúdia

12

Badia d'Alcúdia

S'Albufera

713

Ca'n Picafort

Inca

12

Santa Margalida

Artà

Capdepera

12

Cap Capdepera

3301

15

3320

Cap d'es Pinar

15

4030

15

Manacor

4020

Punta de Amer

Porreres

14

Felanitx

5120

19

Campos

19

Santanyí

9

Cap nes

Celler Ca'n Ripoll

Founded in 1768, this fantastic restaurant has been going for centuries — just step inside the door for a quick journey back in time! The huge stone-columned archways, and even larger wine vats, old copper pots, decorative

plates and implements hanging around the walls give it tremendous character. It is not cheap, but certainly worth visiting – and the food is excellent.

CELLER CA'N RIPOLL
C/ Jaume Armengol 4, 07300 Inca
(971 500024, fax 971 880063
www.canripoll.com
daily ex Sun/holidays and Feb, from 13.30-16.30 and 20.30-11.45 €€€

starters such as salads, asparagus, hors d'oeuvres, and typical local dishes like **tumbet, frito Mallorquín, snails, arròs brut**, **paella**, etc

meat dishes can be roast **suckling pig**, oven-roast lamb or **kid**, lamb chops, pork, chicken

other dishes include **stuffed aubergines, omelettes, seafood**

for **dessert**: almond cake, cheesecake, ice creams, sorbets, crème caramel

The **Celler Sa Travessa** at C/ Murta 16 ((971 500049; €-€€) is similar to Ca'n Ripoll (you can still eat surrounded by huge wine vats), but smaller and more economical. Good Mallorcan cooking here too, with similar dishes to Ca'n Ripoll. It has a very attractive small shady patio for hot weather.

restaurants

eat

Transport: operators and websites

Only details of operators' websites are shown here, together with any important notes. See the operators' websites for full timetables, or collect printed timetables from a tourist office or the train/bus station when you arrive.

Web sites

1 • Sóller train *and* tram: www.trendesoller.com (click the Union flag).

2 • Inca train line: http://tib.caib.es. Click the Union flag, then train symbol, to download timetables.

3 • All buses: http://tib.caib.es. Click the Union flag, then the bus symbol, to download timetables by zone (lines 100, 200, etc).

4 • Sa Calobra boats: www.barcosazules.com. Click the Union flag

---

Excursion 1: websites 1, 3 and 4. **Note:** There may be extra boats from Sa Calobra on busy summer days, but *do not rely on this.* If you miss the last boat, call RadioTaxi Escorca. If you miss the last train, a bus (℡ 971 630301) departs Port Sóller for Palma at half past every hour until 19.30 (21.30 summer).

Walk 1: website 1 for train; website 3 for bus

Walk 2: website 3

Walk 3 and 4*: website 1 for train; website 3 for bus

Walks 5* and 6: website 1 for train; website 3 for bus (to go); website 2 (to return)

Walks 7 and 8: website 1 for train; website 3 for bus

Walk 9: website 3. *NB:* return bus L140 departs Galilea 14.20, 18.05 Mon-Fri, but only *on demand at weekends* (℡ 971 430515 until 19.00 the day before travel)

Walk 10: frequent city buses from the Plaça d'Espanya

Excursion 2: website 2

*Another way to get to Walks 4 and 5 is to take a train to Bunyola, then bus L221 to Orient; departs Bunyola daily at 10.00 (09.45 Sat.), but must be booked in advance; ℡ 971 615219 up until 19.00 the day before travel.

TRANSPORT

Food intolerances are becoming ever more common, and even for those who have learned to cope at home, it can be daunting to go on holiday. *Will the food in restaurants be safe? Will I be able to buy gluten- and dairy-free foods?* If you suffer from food intolerance you have probably already learned at home that what initially seems a penance in fact becomes a challenge and eventually a joy. You eat far healthier meals, with fewer additives. Nowhere is this more enjoyable than around the Mediterranean and on Mallorca, where olive oil, fish, tomatoes and 'alternative' grains and flours are basic to the diet. Many, many dishes are *naturally* gluten- and dairy-free..

EATING IN RESTAURANTS

The most common **first courses** are soups, fish and salads. As you can see from the starters recipes in the book, most are perfectly safe — for instance, paella, *arròs brut* or other rice-based soups, stuffed aubergines or avocados, and most fish courses. If you want to try *pa amb oli,* why not? Take (or buy) your own bread (preferably a dark, country-style loaf), and ask them to replace the cheese with more meat, if cheese is a problem.

   Main courses are mentioned on page 7 — fish and seafood, often grilled, roasts of pork, lamb and pig. Sauces *(salsas)* usually consist of wine, tomatoes, onions, herbs and garlic, all reduced rather than thickened with

EAT GF, DF

wheat flour (as you can see from my recipes). If you are a sauce addict, it is safer to *ask* (see inside back flap for help in Spanish, although the staff usually speak English). *Fried* fish is invariably dusted with flour (otherwise it is more difficult to cook), but *ask:* they may be happy to do it for you without flour. All my recommended restaurants cook meals individually; the staff are always accessible.

For **sweets**, try the gf, df almond cake and ice cream (page 49) — a Mallorcan speciality, on the menu in so many restaurants. Everyone offers fruit (including many 'exotics'); some have gf, df chocolate dishes (made with dark chocolate); *ask!*

SELF-CATERING

While many hotels on the island can cater for food intolerances — or will let you use their fridges (just label your container), consider self-catering (see page 15), so that you can try some of my recipes with the *authentic local* ingredients.

Gf, df shopping

Most of the large supermarkets have a 'natural foods' section, but the choice is usually limited to soya or rice milks and puddings. In the panel on page 18 you'll find a list of shops offering all the gf, df foods you need. But do experiment with some of the various grains on offer in the Mercat de L'Olivar!

Pulses and dried fruits in the Mercat de L'Olivar

Gf, df cooking

You can make all the **recipes** in this book using gluten- and dairy-free ingredients. The Sunflower team have tested them using a 1:1 substitution; the cooking *method* was unchanged.

Flour (for baking and white sauces) can be replaced with 'gf flour' — or corn, rice, potato or chick-pea flour. If you are not able to find soya 'cream', plain soya yoghurt is suitable for the recipes calling for cream — including biscuit glacé on page 29.

A few recipes call for cheese: for the house salad (page 29) we just substituted chopped tofu or ham; for the lasagne (page 80) we substituted an extra layer of tomato slices on top (but could have used soya vegan cheese slices).

Take advantage of almonds on Mallorca: ground almonds are a delicious coating for frying fish, and even better when you grind them fresh yourself!

CONVERSION TABLES

Weights		Volume		Oven temperatures		
						gas
				°C	°F	mark
10 g	1/2 oz	15 ml	1 tbsp			
25 g	1 oz	55 ml	2 fl oz	140°C	275°F	1
50 g	2 oz	75 ml	3 fl oz	150°C	300°F	2
110 g	4 oz	150 ml	1/4 pt	170°C	325°F	3
200 g	7 oz	275 ml	1/2 pt	180°C	350°F	4
350 g	12 oz	570 ml	1 pt	190°C	375°F	5
450 g	1 lb	1 l	1-3/4 pt	200°C	400°F	6
700 g	1 lb 8 oz	1.5 l	2-1/2 pt	220°C	425°F	7
900 g	2 lb			230°C	430°F	8
1.35 g	3 lb			240°C	475°F	9

MENU ITEMS

aceitunas olives
acelgas Swiss chards
agua water
 con gas sparkling
 sin gas still
aguacate avocado
ajo garlic
alcachofas artichokes
almendras almonds
arroz rice
 arròs brut see page 93
asado/a roasted
atún tuna
bacalau dried salted cod
berenjenas aubergines
bocadillo sandwich
brossat ricotta-like cheese (also a cheesecake)
caballa mackerel
cabrito kid
café coffee
calamares squid
calabacín marrow
cangrejo crab
caracoles snails
carne meat
cebollas onions
cerdo pork
cerveza beer

champiñones mushrooms
chuleta, costilla chop or cutlet
coca cake
cocarrois see page 113
col cabbage
conejo rabbit
cordero lamb
del día daily special
dorada bream
empanadas meat pies
escudella vegetable soup
espinacas spinach
espada swordfish
frit mariner see page 81
frito/a fried
 frito Mallorquín see page 81
gambas prawns
guisantes peas
harina flour, usually wheat
helado ice cream
higado liver
higos figs
huevos eggs
jamón ham
 serrano air dried ham
lagosta lobster
langostinos crayfish,

large prawns
leche milk
lechona suckling pig
limón lemon
lomo loin
lubina sea bass
manzana apple
mantequilla butter
mariscos shellfish
mejillones mussels
melón melon
merluza hake
mero grouper
miel honey
mussola shark
nata cream
nuezes nuts
pa amb oli see pages 7, 37
pan bread
panceta pork belly
parrilla (a la) grilled
pastel pie or cake
patatas potatoes
pescado fish
pimientos peppers
piñones pine nuts
pollo chicken
pulpo octopus
queso cheese
rape monkfish
relleno/a stuffed
riñones kidneys
salmonetes red mullet
salsa sauce

setas wild mushrooms
sobrasada cured pork sausage
sopa soup
sopas Mallorquinas see page 39
tarta tarte, pie
té tea
ternera beef
tintorera shark
tocino bacon
tostado/a toasted
torta cake
trempó see page 47
tumbet see page 57
trigo wheat
vegetales vegetables
verduras greens
vino wine (see page 9)
 dulce sweet
 seco dry
zumo juice

SHOPPING TERMS for the recipes in this book

a bottle of... *una botella de...*
a kilo of... *un kilo de....*

GLOSSARY

half a kilo of...
  medio kilo de...
a bag una bolsa
apples manzanas
almonds almendras
apricots albaricoques
artichokes alcachofas
aubergines berenjenas
avocados aguacates
bacon tocino (or 'béicon')
basil albahaca
bay leaves hojas de laurel
beef* carne de buey
beer cerveza
brandy coñac
bread pan
broccoli brocolí (or brécol)
butter mantequilla
cabbage col
carrots zanahórias
capers alcaparras
cauliflower coliflor
celery, green apio verde
cheese queso
  ricotta-style brossat
chicken pollo
chives cebolleta
chocolate chocolate
cider sidra
cinnamon canela
cod (salted, dry) bacalao

coffee café
crabmeat sticks palitos de cangrejo, palitos de mar
cream nata
custard apples chirimoyas
duck pato
eggs huevos
fennel hinojo
figs higos (dried figs higos secos)
fish pescado
flour harinha
  corn de maíz
  wheat de trigo
fruit fruta
game caza
garlic ajo
ham jamón
  air dried jamón serrano
herbs hierbas
honey miel
ice cream helado
juice zumo
lamb* cordero
lard manteca
leeks puerros
lemons limones
lettuce lechuga
liver higado
marrow calabacín
mayonnaise mahonesa
melon melón
milk leche
mushrooms champiñones
  wild setas

mussels mejillones
mustard mostaza
nuts nueces
olive oil aceite de oliva
olives aceitunas
onions cebollas
  spring sofrito
orange liqueur licor de naranja
oranges naranjas
oregano orégano
parsley perejil
peas guisantes
pepper, black pimienta negra
peppers (green, red) pimientos (verdes, rojos)
pig, suckling lechona
pine nuts piñones
pork* cerdo
potatoes patatas
poultry volatería
prawns gambas (or langostinos)
pulses legumbres
rabbit (hare) conejo (liebre)
rice arroz
rosemary romero
salt sal
sauce salsa
sausage sobresada
shark steaks mussola (Mallorquín) bifsteks de tintorera (Spanish)
snails caracoles
soup sopa
spinach espinacas

spices, condiments condimentos
squid calamares
stock caldo
sugar azúcar
sultanas sultanas
Swiss chards acelgas
tea té
thyme tomillo
tomatoes tomates
tuna atún
turkey pavo
turmeric curcuma
vegetables vegetales
  greens verduras
vinegar vinagre
wine vino
  dry seco
  sweet dulce
walnuts nueces
water água
  plain sem gás
  sparkling com gás

*cuts of meat
chops chuletas (or costillas)
filet filete
leg pierna; chicken legs muslos de pollo
liver hígado
loin lomo
minced meat carne picada
shoulder paletilla
small pieces trozos pequeños
steaks bifsteks

bold type: photograph; *italic type:* map

INDEX

Fourth edition © 2016
Published by Sunflower Books
PO Box 36061, London SW7 3WS
www.sunflowerbooks.co.uk

All rights reserved. No part of this publication may be reproduced, stored in a
retrieval system, or transmitted by any form or by any means, electronic,
mechanical, photocopying, recording or otherwise, without the prior written
permission of the publishers.

ISBN 978-1-85691-464-2

Cover photograph: Resting in the shade

Photos: page 126: Javier Collados; 20, 23, 43, 49, 104, 122, 128: John Under-
    wood; 44, 64, cover: Shutterstock; all others: Julian Crespí, Valerie Crespí Green
Maps: Sunflower Books, adapted from 1:25,000 and 1:50,000 maps published by
    the Instituto Geográfico del Ejército, Madrid
Series design: Jocelyn Lucas
Cookery editor: Marina Bayliss
A CIP catalogue record for this book is available from the British Library.
Printed and bound in England by Short Run Press, Exeter

Before you go ...
log on to
www.sunflowerbooks.co.uk
and click on '**updates**', to see if we have been notified of any changes to
the routes or restaurants.

When you return ...
do let us know if any routes have changed because of road-building, storm
damage or the like. Have any of our restaurants closed — or any new ones
opened *on the route of the walk*? (Not Palma restaurants, please; these books
are not intended to be complete restaurant guides!)
Send your comments to info@sunflowerbooks.co.uk

144 OYSTER BAY - EAST NORWICH PUBLIC LIBRARY
OYSTER BAY, N.Y.
APR 19 2016   3|17-1 L4|19-6.